In 1975, Dan Docherty, a young Scots law graduate and karate black belt, left Glasgow to spend nine years as a Hong Kong police inspector.

As well as serving as a detective and vice squad commander, he also took up Tai Chi and won the 5th Southeast Asian Chinese Full Contact Championships in Malaysia in 1980.

In 1985, he was awarded a postgraduate diploma in Chinese from Ealing College.

He travels extensively teaching Tai Chi and has written four books on the subject.

This book is dedicated to all my mentors and to my son,
Ronan Rene Docherty.

Dan Docherty

WILD COLONIAL BOY

TALES OF A KUNG FU COP

AUSTIN MACAULEY PUBLISHERS™

LONDON • CAMBRIDGE • NEW YORK • SHARJAH

ISBN 9781528991957 (Paperback)
ISBN 9781528991964 (Hardback)
ISBN 9781528991971 (ePub e-book)

www.austinmacauley.com

First Published (2020)
Austin Macauley Publishers Ltd
25 Canada Square
Canary Wharf
London
E14 5LQ

Thanks to my friends, Dave Sweeny, ex-Royal Canadian Mounted Police, and to Peter Mok Bun, ex-Royal Hong Kong Police, for their ideas and suggestions and to Titch for help with production.

Young Dan

I am the eldest of eight boys and two girls born to a couple of Catholic doctors in Glasgow, Scotland, in 1954.

At home, there was a pill for every problem. Whisky with sleeping pills for my dad every night.

All adult members of the family called me 'Young Dan' to distinguish me from my father whose exact name I bore 'Daniel Joseph Docherty'. He was known as 'Doctor Dan'. He was the type who'd send back a perfectly good bottle of wine saying it was corked when he had difficulty telling white from red.

My father was almost 6' tall. In his youth, he'd been a football goalkeeper and a sprinter. He was a heavy smoker. He started out on cigarettes, but switched to cigars when he got into politics. He drank every day, mainly mediocre blended Scotch. My mother was 5'8" and big boned. She never smoked, but would have a drink to be sociable. They were a team, but my mother was the brains.

My father took an early interest in my education. He called me into his home surgery one Sunday and handed me a tome entitled, 'The Spell Well Word Book'. He also produced a leather punishment strap and told me he'd test my spelling every Sunday and he'd belt me for each mistake. I very quickly became good at spelling.

He told me that being the oldest [of 10 kids eventually], he would hold me responsible for anything my siblings did wrong. Very Chinese, 'The hammer hits the nail; the nail hits the wood.' I don't consider that I was abused. I just never particularly liked my parents and from as early as I can remember, I only ever addressed them as 'you'.

We only had a radio until I was about six, when we acquired a TV. Our parents sent us kids to bed at 8.30 pm after we'd said our prayers. If we made a noise or if I was caught reading a book after lights out, my father would give me a smack. He rarely left a mark.

The only time when music was heard in the house was if our maid and baby sitter, kind Mrs Lochrie, brought along her son's hi fi and a bunch of records.

Clan Docherty

My father sometimes took me for private lessons with his dad, Michael Docherty, a gruff, but mischievous ex-headmaster, whom we respectfully addressed as 'Granda'. He always seemed to want to teach me Russian fables or incomprehensible arithmetic. Sometimes, he'd tell me about his times in the Royal Navy during the First World War, about the Battle of Jutland and the use of 'Q' ships.

On holiday, he'd sometimes play football with us and every Sunday after we'd been to the swimming baths, we'd visit him and our Grandma. Even when he was dying of cancer, he'd always have our pocket money ready on the table beside the bed.

His wife, Ellen Stewart, was a pleasant lady who made excellent fruit pies. She'd often have a book for me, much too advanced for my age, I'd read them anyway. They had five sons. Louis was killed in a tram accident, as a result we never had bicycles.

They were very proud of their eldest son, Captain James Docherty, Royal Army Medical Corps, who was blown to Kingdom come in 1944 by the Nazis at Monte Cassino. In the summer of 1971, my parents took all of us to Italy. Grandma Docherty came too. We went to Rome, Vatican City, Capri and Sorrento. I also went with my Grandma, my father, my brothers James and John to the war cemetery at Minturno, where Uncle James was buried next to his best chum, a Church of England padre.

Archbishop Scanlan of Glasgow had arranged a private audience for the entire Docherty clan with Pope Paul VI at his summer residence, Castel Gandolfo, just outside Rome. I had the chance to chat with him personally for a couple of minutes.

When Uncle James went off with the 8th Army to the war in North Africa, my father was a medical student by day and at night served as an air raid warden when the German planes came to bomb the Glasgow shipyards. He was goalkeeper for Cambridge University soccer team and served in the Royal Air Force as Medical Officer to Kings Flight.

Many years later at a big function, my dad was introduced as Doctor Dan Docherty to war hero, Group Captain Sir Douglas Bader (a notoriously rude fellow). Bader came out with 'Another damn quack eh?

My father replied, "Another damn ex RAF quack if you please."

My Uncle Michael was a Jesuit seminarian when he was called up. He was a Sergeant in Army Intelligence based in the Middle East. He later became an expert in photography and radiography. He could handle himself too, one time up in Loch Katrine, I saw Uncle Mike put my dad in an armlock. It was obvious, he knew what he was doing.

He drank more heavily after his wife died. After years of living in London, he moved back to Glasgow to live with his mother. It seems Captain James Docherty's war medals disappeared after Uncle Mike moved in, but what does it matter?

I hadn't seen Uncle Mike for quite a while, when I heard he was dying of cancer, so I went to visit him with my brother, Steve. He was in a bad way. I talked to him of old army times in Jordan. The handshake was extra tight at the end, we both knew it was the last time.

The youngest Docherty brother was my genius Uncle John, the psychiatrist, who had served as a Captain in the RAMC of whom more later.

My grandmother always had a glass of Benedictine liqueur when she came to visit us. She was one of those nice ladies who supported church bazaars, but she had a Belfast edge to her. One time, at my parents' house in front of Uncle

Mike, she talked about her 'three fine sons', meaning the three who had become doctors.

I liked Uncle Mike who was an expert in radiography. He didn't deserve this crap.

All the brothers were valiant.

Clan Kennedy

My Grandpa, Andrew Kennedy, was an easy going, but burly gent who enjoyed drinking whisky, smoking cigarettes and betting on the horses and dogs. He didn't seem to know any Russian fables, but he could do tricks with matchsticks and would take me to the swings when I was four.

He met his end when he was hit by a truck on his way to the bookmakers from the pub, most likely, he was smoking a cigarette at the time.

His wife, Sarah Parker, an ex-flapper, who smoked cigarettes and drank sherry or gin, worked in a second hand store. We called her Gran. Their first son, Ignatius, was a science graduate who became a priest. Son Andrew was a college lecturer who had worked in Kuwait for a few years. Daughter Rita was a school teacher. Sheila was a headmistress. She didn't get married, but was kind and gentle to all. My mother was the oldest girl. Her aunts were mainly infant school teachers and they were probably quite put out when she broke with tradition and became a doctor. Nobody likes a smartass.

The Dochertys are prone to mockery, are somewhat mercurial and have a wiry strength. The Kennedys were calmer creatures who liked comfort, they have a burly strength. Extroverts and introverts. Fire, and water.

All Xmas and birthday presents involving guns or excitement would come from my father, my mother was the censor. My earliest roommate, James, was artistic but practical. He could fix things, make things.

I just collected Airfix tiny model soldiers. I particularly liked my blue plastic French Foreign Legionnaires. However, my legionnaires remained entirely blue (including the kepis) because I had no skill or patience with a painting brush.

Summer Holidays

As a Glasgow City Councillor, my father was entitled to book a two weeks summer break for the family at one of the Council's cottages in the scenic area around Loch Lomond known as the Trossachs. The 'cottages' were huge, but old-fashioned, set around the shores of Loch Katrine, which supplies Glasgow with water. My grandparents would come too. They'd drink gin and tonics together in the afternoons enjoying the views of the loch and the hills. After dinner they would play cards.

I enjoyed going for walks on the private roads around the loch. We could play bowls or go putting. Sometimes we'd row around the vast loch in the old, somewhat clumsy boats that were available. On Sundays, I was the altar boy for my uncle, Father Ignatius Kennedy.

It was a magical place, Rob Roy Macgregor Campbell, rebel (he took part in the 1715 rebellion) and cattle rustler was born and died close to the loch. There is a lovely islet known as 'Ellen's Isle' in the loch and sometimes we'd row over and make a landing. There was also a 'steamer' called 'The Sir Walter Scott' which kept the cottages in contact with civilisation. It still makes daily cruises.

I'm a bookworm and in the course of one summer vacation, I read all of Sir Walter Scott's Waverley novels. The main protagonist always seemed to be a callow youth who falls in with desperate characters. With a bit of luck, he might find a mentor amongst them…

The author celebrates his First Communion with Aunt Sheila and Mother.

Convent School

From the ages of five to eight, I attended Merrylee Franciscan Convent School. I was made school captain at the age of six. I liked to think that my father being Convenor of the City of Glasgow Education Committee, Senior Magistrate and Deputy Lord Provost played no part in my elevation, which was based solely on merit.

As school captain, I had to wear a red ribbon over my shoulder. That was ok. Getting girls aged up to eight years of age to obey me, proved surprisingly difficult even though I always wore my red ribbon.

I had my first fighting epiphany when playing soccer in the Convent playground. Severino got mad at me and took the ball for a throw in. I was standing nearby and realised that he was going to try to throw the ball directly at me, so I stepped in and punched him on the nose as he arched his back prior to throwing the ball. It was so easy to hit him, so natural. Hey nun girls, I don't make the rules

I got away with that one, but the school was strict and believed in corporal punishment. The teachers: Sister Mary Claire the headmistress, whose grammar lessons I remember even now. Sister Mary Imelda, Miss Harrigan and Mrs Bartholomew, belted my hands for various faults and misdemeanours. In addition, I had my water pistol confiscated. This thoroughly deserved belting stood me in good stead years later in life. Or did it?

Mrs Bartholomew was a twit, always boasting how she was a 'holy terror' and how she was the only person to know Mam Sodhail was the highest mountain in Scotland. It isn't. Also I want that water pistol back.

I enjoyed Miss Harrigan's Scottish Highland Dancing, especially the Sword Dance. For the reels, we boys got to choose their partners. There were some fine young ladies. I always chose Patti H to be my partner, she was the loveliest of all. She was probably the best dancer too.

Ogilvie an Ogilvie

After three years of nuns, I passed the entry exam for John Ogilvie Hall. Ogilvie was a Jesuit martyr converted from Calvinism and canonised in 1976, Scotland's only Post Reformation saint.

The exam included dictation of a passage referring to junks and sampans. Each year's student intake was divided equally between Ogilvie House and Gonzaga. I was in Ogilvie. I had a female class teacher for the first two years.

Academically, I was not outstanding, but one Friday, Miss Magee announced the results of our class test saying, "Well that's a surprise, Daniel Docherty is top of the class this week."

She belted me once. It was not justified.

It was in her classroom that I first noticed maps of the world had huge areas marked off in a reddish pink. Apparently, they were part of something called the British Empire or Commonwealth. There were regular collections of pennies for 'the black babies'. Somehow all this was connected.

We learned that British people were very kind to other nations, especially British colonies and helped educate and civilise them as well as introducing them to Christianity and the concept of 'fair play'.

In Primary 5, worried by my seeming lethargy in her classes, Miss Sweeney called in my parents as she thought I wasn't getting enough sleep. Truth was that I found her classes boring.

I never understood music, musical instruments, opera or singing at all. One day, Miss Bowers, the music teacher stopped the class and told me I am tone deaf. From the age of eight, I was banned from singing with the class.

My first male teacher was Bill Tollan, later to become a priest. He ran the rugby and cricket clubs. We were a posh school, so we didn't play soccer competitively, but only for fun at break time.

The headmaster, Thomas Burke, was old style. Every weekend, we were given a passage to analyse. We were expected to know the meaning of every word. Burke would go round the class on Monday morning testing us word by word. If a student didn't know a word, he had to come out from behind his desk, put his hands out and Burke would give him one stroke of the belt.

One time I made him laugh though when I defined the word 'gait' as 'the parts of a woman we hadn't yet talked about.' Burke laughed so much, he couldn't belt anyone that lesson.

Aged 11, I was an accomplished bullshitter.

I was attacked once at the school gate by a boy called Hilley, who was a year older than me. His nice elder brother was trying to stop us fighting when their dad and mine arrived in their cars at the same time. It turned out that they were old pals.

Burke let us off with a warning. He knew my dad and Granda.

I played for the school rugby and cricket teams. I wasn't that skilful, but was good at making and breaking tackles when playing rugby and hitting batsmen with the cricket ball when bowling.

Sectarianism

Scottish schools were divided into Catholic and non-Catholic. That remains the case today. When I was a boy, religious sectarianism was rife, every rugby game was a mini tribal war against the 'Prods' and 'Blue Noses', epithets used by my dad to refer to Protestants and supporters of Glasgow Rangers Football Club – of which my great Grandad – a Protestant Stewart from Belfast, had been the head groundsman. Just to even things up, my great grandfather from Donegal was a friend of Irish rebel, Michael Collins, and kept a safe house for him in Glasgow. Nearly, all the Protestant schools wore blue rugby shirts like the Scottish team, we were in green and gold. Celtic, the Catholic football club wore green and white hooped shirts. Go figure.

Comics

When I was about 11, I came back from school one day to find my parents in the room I shared with three of my brothers. They were ripping up my entire collection of super hero comics. They told me that I should only be reading school books.

I understood that they were trying to do their best for 10 children born over a period of 11 years. My mother also had a couple of miscarriages. Even so.

I made sure both my kids had comics. I especially liked the Silver Surfer. Not exactly a sanctimonious Captain America type, nor yet a cackling psychopath like Doctor Viktor von Doom, the Surfer had his own truth and was much misunderstood.

My parents were inconsistent though and one year for my Christmas, my father gave me PC Wren's French Foreign Legion trilogy, Beau Geste, Beau Sabreur and Beau Ideal. I was fascinated by the characters and by French language and culture. Around the same time, I got into Dumas. I liked Cardinal Richelieu, but thought D'Artagnan was a klutz.

The College

At the age of 12, I was admitted to Saint Aloysius College, a posh, Jesuit high school. My father, his brothers and both my grandfathers had all attended the school. My father had been school captain. When I started at the College, he was Chairman of the Board of Governors. No pressure. The school motto was *Ad Maiorem Natus Sum'* (I was born for greater things), while the motto of the Jesuits was *Ad Maiora Dei Gloria'* (To the Greater Glory of God). Calling the school aspirational was an understatement.

Each year, St Aloysius had an intake of about 100 new boys. For the first couple of years, we were streamed into A / B/ C in accordance with academic ability. I was at the upper end of B stream. I represented the school at rugby and cricket.

At the College, we had to attend Mass at St Aloysius Parish Church every morning before school started. We had to attend a Benediction service every Friday afternoon. We went to Confession on Saturday evenings and to early morning mass on Sundays. I was attending church eight days a week.

Father Gerard Manley Hopkins, one of the first of the modern poets, had been based in the St Aloysius parish house. I taught myself his poem, 'Inversnaid' because I had been there on holidays and loved the place, on the banks of Loch Lomond. Hopkins was the only Jesuit I ever liked. Their cloaks and gowns and lack of humour reminded me of Dracula.

Academically I had three great teachers for three to four years; Teddy Tolan for maths, Bruno Filetti for French and, best of all, Bob Crampsey, for history. All were no bullshit alpha males, strict but excellent and humorous teachers.

In those days, everyone in Scotland knew of Bob Crampsey. As well as being head of the history department at the College, he was a sports commentator for the popular TV show, Scotsport, was a former BBC Brain of Britain contest winner, journalist and Churchill scholar. I still have my old history notes in my Chinese rosewood desk. It was an honour to have him as my cricket coach.

As a youth, I watched too much TV – mostly Westerns and espionage. Invariably, my favourite characters were iconic loners with a penchant for getting into trouble (Danger Man, Have Gun Will Travel, Man in a Suitcase, Rawhide, Callan…). Almost all the trouble seemed to revolve around women or guns, sometimes both.

Doc and the Glasgow Kiss

At St. Aloysius, I had occasional fights. One time when I was 13, a 15-year-old boy attempted to give me a 'Glasgow Kiss'. Often people get a broken nose when attacked with a head butt, but instinctively, I went forward and my assailant hit his nose on my forehead. He came off second best.

In the school rugby team, my mission was usually to target one of the skilful opposition players. The boys all called me 'Doc.'

I liked that because one of my heroes is Doc Holliday who was dying of consumption but still backed his pals the Earps at the OK Corral. For a while, I wanted to be a dentist, just didn't have the science.

The Mermaid

For some months, I had a Canadian French teacher called Pierre A. He told us a joke. Two guys are fishing in a little boat when one of them gets a tug on his line. After a struggle, he reels in his catch and sits it on his lap.

It's a beautiful mermaid. The lucky fisherman looks her up and down, then suddenly throws the mermaid back into the water.

His astonished friend asked, "Why?"

The fisherman replied, "Not why, how?"

Mermaids are fish from the waist down.

Glasgow Mermaid

My dance partner from convent days, Patti H, had a big sister called Jackie who was a year older. She attended a Catholic School for girls just across the road from the College.

One day just after the school bells had been rung for the day, I found her blocking my path. She fluttered her eyes and gave me a husky hello. I attempted to walk round her so she grabbed the sleeve of my school blazer and spoke again.

"I said hello."

Her school skirt was a little too short, her shoes were heeled. She looked really sexy, but I knew she would be trouble and a very dangerous diversion. Better just throw her back in.

After my final exams, I stayed till the end of term. I needn't have worried Admission to Glasgow University required a minimum of three B grade passes and a C grade. I was awarded A grades in English and History, B grades in Maths and French and a C grade in Latin. I had passed with ease.

Hypocrite Father
Hypocrite Son

My father was Convenor of the Glasgow City Council Education Committee and was being called a hypocrite in public because he had to enforce a socialist agenda of cutting off grants to fee-paying schools when he was sending me and my nine siblings to fee-paying schools. The Docherty clan was not popular with fellow students or their parents or their teachers. During my last term, I was insulted and assaulted by classmates, my brothers John and Des were bullied.

My brothers were lined up to follow in my footsteps to the College while my sisters the fiery (but good person), Rosemary and the gentler Alex attended Notre Dame Convent School, I told my father to take all nine out of feepaying schools. He did so. One of the few times, he actually listened to me.

When I was 16, during a practice game of rugby, I had my hand stamped on by a schoolmate when I was trapped at the bottom of a ruck. I thought it a cheap shot and never played rugby again after that. I always tried to follow a code of never fouling or taking cheap shots at opponents, but if they did something to me or one of my friends, I would do something to them. I passed this code to my kids. If you let others hurt you and do nothing about it, then they'll do it again and yet others may join them.

Confucius once said, "Kill one to warn a hundred."

Granda Docherty used to say, "One door shuts, another one closes." How right he was.

Karate – Danny X 3

The key to success in life is being in the right place at the right time.

One Saturday afternoon, I was sitting with my mother in her car at Bellahouston Sports Centre waiting to pick up my brother John from training (he was a Scottish international hurdler) when we noticed some guys wearing white pyjamas with various coloured belts doing karate. My mother said that as I was going to start university in a few months, I should take up some sport, what about this karate stuff. At the sports centre the following week, I signed up for karate.

A bespectacled guy called Danny Thomson wearing a green belt took the Saturday class. He was pleasant and skilful. The Sunday and Tuesday classes were run by a guy in his late 30s called Al Doran, an ex-paratrooper-turned director of a furniture company and a guy called Danny Bryceland in his late 20s, who had been British and European Kumite (fighting) Champion. Al Doran was a fourth degree black belt and ran the club, handling the licensing and admin. Danny was a 3rd degree black belt and the top fighter.

The style of karate they taught was called Shotokan. It was direct, linear and expansive with long low stances. The first Japanese master I encountered was Keinosuke Enoeda, who was fast, strong and had excellent technique. Enoeda was hard, but generally fair. I attended courses given by other Japanese Shotokan masters, but they were not Enoeda's level.

A few months after I started training, there was a Scotland vs. England karate tournament in Glasgow. I went along and was enthused by the fights and demos, especially the unorthodox Kumite demonstrated by the late great Gary Spiers – headbutts and all. It became something to aspire to.

When I'd been training for just over a year, I got talking to some other young guys with similar inexperience and we went to see Al and asked if we could take part in the free Kumite in the Scottish Championships in Dundee, even though we'd never actually been taught free Kumite.

Al probably thought we were all talk. Five kids each with about one year training and no Kumite experience taking on all comers – even black belts.

If He Moves, Hit Him

We entered individually and as a five-man team. I was a purple belt and was drawn against a skinny yellow belt in the individual Kumite. I had listened to the senior grades with respect and tried to aim each technique within two inches of the opponent's body. My opponent hit me twice to the body and won the fight. I hadn't got a scratch on me, hadn't scored any points. Anti-climax.

In the team event, I was drawn against a black belt Scottish International karate team member. I didn't want to let my team buddies down and knew I had to come up with something. I decided every time he moved I'd try to hit him. I did so. I didn't score any points, but I drew the fight and the other guys in the team were happy. In those days everyone called me 'Danny'.

1973 – the author [foreground]training karate under Sensei Al Doran.

Nanbu

Came a time when I was something like fourth kyu (purple and white belt) and we couldn't get a Japanese Shotokan master to give us a course and grading, instead Al arranges for a Japanese master based in Paris to come over. This guy, Nanbu, turns up wearing baggy white karate trousers, shades and a little half smile that never left him.

We'd never seen stuff like this before. We were doing spinning back kicks, hook kicks, spinning leg sweeps, jump kicks, techniques against multiple opponents. His English wasn't great, but one word he kept using was 'Escape!' Above all, else he taught us footwork and evasion.

He had great technique, excellent timing. He was fast and you couldn't read him.

He came from a Samurai family. His dad had been a Judo instructor to the Japanese navy while his granddad had been a Sumo Yokozuna (Grand Champion). Nanbu had studied Judo then Kendo. He went on to train in Shito-ryu Karate and became Japanese University Champion.

Subsequently Henri Plee, the father of European Karate, brought Nanbu to France where he competed against the top French exponents and invariably won. At that time, it was unheard of for a Japanese to compete against Westerners. Eventually, Nanbu became coach to the French karate team. They beat the Japanese in Japan.

Nanbu went on to form his own style which he called Sankukai (Association of the Three Elements – Mind, Body and Spirit). It was clear that this was something more than just karate, there were strong elements of Kendo and Aikido as well. Nanbu was also highly skilled in traditional Japanese weapons.

Tai Chi elder brother Ian Cameron from Edinburgh told me that in the 70s he went to see a big karate event in Glasgow. The old Japanese masters like Suzuki of Wado Ryu sat stony faced as a bare chested Nanbu gave a Nunchaku demo while chanting Japanese poetry. Class.

Before meeting Nanbu, I always went for the 'Big Hit'. Nanbu had the French attitude. He did things with panache, brio, finesse and elegance. It wasn't enough anymore to just whack folk, though it remained an option.

My fascination with martial arts led me to buy magazines and a vast (still growing) collection of books on Chinese and Japanese culture.

I bought all Nanbu's books. They were all in French.

Pas probleme…

Glasgow Confucianism

Nanbu spars with Danny Bryceland, former British Kumite team member in the World Championships. Makes Danny look like a beginner. Nanbu was the reason the club split in two. Almost all the senior grades followed Danny Bryceland to go back to Shotokan. I knew Danny was better than Al at karate, but I preferred Al as a man and he had become something of a mentor to me, I stayed loyal to him.

After a while, I started helping Al by teaching the beginners. I'm sorry to say that I used brutality to teach them because I had seen Japanese Sensei do the same. Anyone who made a mistake, I'd hit them or sweep them to the floor. It was the culture I was used to at school and at home. The belt and the fist – Glasgow Confucianism, 'kill the chicken to warn the monkey.' I became Red Pole enforcer at home for my siblings and at the karate club.

I slowly realised that Nanbu never used brutality when instructing.

I stopped hurting beginners unless they were a danger to themselves or others. The Sunday, after Nanbu's seminar, when Al asked me to take the beginners, I started working on the sidestep with them. From that day until this except for the occasional psycho (sometimes they only understand and even go looking for pain); I tried not to hurt anyone, well, most of the time.

Nanbu showed me that martial arts can be fun and convinced me that my interest in practicing and teaching martial arts could be a viable alternative career, I didn't have to be a lawyer. But how to do it?

Around this time, my kid brothers, Andy (later to be a Lt. Colonel in Army Intelligence) and Steve (who became a landscape gardener), started going with me every Saturday to the junior karate class. Al's daughter ran the class and I assisted.

Our grandmother (on our mother's side) and our kind Aunt Sheila lived a few minutes' walk from the karate class, so we'd often visit them before or after training.

My brother Charlie who became a police inspector in Northampton took up judo around the same time, training to brown belt level and started bringing along our shy younger sister, Alex (later managing director of a travel firm).

1974 – Annus Mirabilis
Mr. Docherty's Law

In the summer of 1974, I graduated in law from Glasgow University, but I had little enthusiasm at my graduation ceremony.

In Scottish degree courses, there were certain compulsory subjects and some interesting options. My chosen options included Political Economy, Accountancy and Forensic Medicine which the world's leading pathologists, the Glaisters, a father and son act had taught for decades at Glasgow University.

Their magnum opus on Forensic Pathology and Toxicology was a trailblazer and remains the standard textbook. My father had studied under the younger Glaister, I studied for a year under his successor, Regius Professor of Forensic Medicine Gilbert Forbes, a slightly sinister old gent. I was spellbound by his stories and his insight. There were around nine of us who'd opted for Forensic Medicine. We had to do a written exam then an oral with the intimidating Regius Professor himself

I knocked his door and he barked, "Enter!"

I obeyed forthwith to find Professor Forbes ensconced on a majestic throne in a semi darkness. He pointed to a much humbler chair with lighting above it and on either side.

"Daniel Joseph Docherty, Eh?" he intoned. "Are you perhaps related to 'Doctor Daniel Joseph Docherty', the Chairman of our Glasgow University Court?"

"I'm afraid so, Professor," I replied.

It was the first time I heard him laugh.

I had no trouble getting a pass in Forensic Medicine.

After the graduation ceremony (first and last time I've worn a gown in public), I become a member of the Inner Temple in London, studying by correspondence course for the English bar (Scots law is based on Roman law unlike English law, which is based on precedent), I had to eat three dinners each term at the Inner Temple.

All this cost money.

Altar Boy Dan and Father Ignatius

Because of my Glasgow Law degree, I had exemptions from subjects like Constitutional Law so I had plenty of free time.

I took up playing golf and often did so midweek. My parents encouraged me, as they believed golf would help me make the right contacts when I became a successful lawyer. I just didn't have the finesse golf required, besides which, it is time consuming.

Uncle Ignatius would often invite me to play a round on one of the excellent courses we have in Scotland. He was a quiet, reflective man who also loved detective and espionage novels. He was originally a scientist.

I once asked him why he had become a priest instead of finding a nice wife. He said that women only wanted a meal ticket. As a priest, his food, accommodation and cleaning were all provided and he could afford to run a car, could come and go as he pleased and play golf twice a week. Maybe he had a point. He was intelligent and good company.

Monsieur Docherty – A Scots Black Belt in Paris

Shortly after my graduation, Nanbu awarded me 1st Dan black belt, Al immediately took off his own black belt and tied it around my waist. Al then arranged for me to spend eight days or so in Paris at the renowned dojo of Henri Plee, famous as 'The Father of European karate'.

When I was in Paris, Okinawan Gojuryu (Hard Soft School) Karate Sensei, Seikichi Toguchi, was giving a course at the Plee dojo. It began with his two assistants doing back flips up and down the hall, while Toguchi went through some weird stretching ritual, incredible for a tiny pot-bellied man in his 70s. Toguchi's techniques were subtle and practical, not so different from Tai Chi applications. I also attended classes with Plee's assistants, those guys were understated, but very effective.

In what time I had left, I visited the dojos of Sensei Taiji Kase and top French karate competitor, Dominique Valera. Old time Shotokan, stalwart Kase, was affable and signed his book for me. He let me watch him give a master class in form and application. Unfortunately, I didn't get to meet Valera himself, but his assistant, Daniel Rennesson, was a complete gent and invited me to train with the class. Those guys were so sharp, they could read me almost every time.

I also trained with Nanbu's main Parisian assistants, Tsukada and Kamohara, with whom I sparred, they were skilful and fast. Some of their students were on the French team.

I used to frequent a café, 'Le Celtique', near Plee's dojo and got talking to some French karateka (practitioners) there, who also practiced Tai Chi and who really rated it for improving their karate skills.

On the last night, I asked to meet Monsieur Henri Plee. I was told to wait and was then invited into his office. I gave him a bottle of Chivas Regal whisky. He produced two glasses and asked me to sit down.

I was a nobody, a 20-year-old kid from Glasgow, Plee was a legend. I'd read the stories about him having faced challenges from boxers, wrestlers, Judo masters etc. I knew he was a writer as well as a fighter. Plee was charming as only the French can be and was an amiable raconteur. He said, "Martial arts are like the women, some men are lucky and find the right one for them straight away. Others need to try a few different ones before they find the right one. Then there are the Casanovas of the martial arts, wandering from style to style and teacher to teacher."

It was an honour for me as a callow, near penniless student to drink whisky with the famous Henri Plee at his dojo discussing martial arts and artists. He was funny and quick witted, great company.

The author after receiving his black belt diploma from Sensei Nanbu in 1974.

Bringing It All Back Home

When I got back to Glasgow, my fellow students told me I was twice as fast as before. My Parisian interlude made me realise the importance of getting as much quality tuition as possible and then to practice.

Shortly after this, one of our club members told me of a Tai Chi class in central Glasgow. I started attending. The teacher was a dancer and only knew a short Tai Chi sequence. She was graceful, but it was obvious that she had no idea what she was doing. The books and magazine articles that were available on Tai Chi then were most unconvincing in terms of explaining its martial aspects.

My doctor parents became concerned that their exam-passing son had stopped taking exams. By then I realised that the only way to satisfy my interest, martial arts, was to go to the Far East and see what I could find, but I only had a few hundred pounds in the bank.

Plus Ca Change Ca Change

It all changed rather suddenly.

I chanced upon a recruitment ad in the Observer magazine for inspectors in the Royal Hong Kong Police, 'The proving ground for natural leaders'. The money was good and with my degree, I'd be on the top salary scale. Getting paid to travel to the Far East to learn Chinese. Incredible.

It was a paramilitary police force. If I passed the interview, I'd learn drill, musketry, self-defence and law. I sent in my application. I was called for an initial interview in Edinburgh and had to write my opinions on police officers being armed (no brainer).

One of the interviewers, Superintendent Ron Smith, became my boss two years later, only to die suddenly. He barely made 40. The other interviewer was a Hong Kong Government Administrative Officer who had graduated from Glasgow University. He expressed amazement when I told him I had never taken drugs and never smoked a cigarette, I could never stand the smell of tobacco.

I was asked to attend a final interview and medical in London.

I had to list two referees. Naturally, I chose the excellent Al Doran as one. The other was John Goodfellow my first boss. When the university closed for the summer, I worked as a groundsman in Toryglen Recreation Fields. John was from Wales and had a poverty-stricken childhood. He left school aged eight to work on a farm and did a host of menial jobs till he joined the army. Eventually, he got a job in the recreation fields and became a head groundsman. He was strict, but fair and humorous, the worst thing he ever called me was 'Silly sausage.' He was well respected by the men who worked under him and knew his job inside out.

As we had the same name, my dad always assumed that all mail addressed to D.J. Docherty was for him. He opened the letter about the London interview. Everyone in the family was horrified and did their best to talk me out of it. My father arranged for me to meet City of Glasgow Police Commissioner Sir David McNee, who told me as a graduate entrant in the Glasgow Police, I could be a Sergeant in no time.

No thanks Commissioner. Don't want to be no Glasgow Sergeant.

I had grown disillusioned with my life, my family and the study of law and realised I was better suited to a more active life on every level. I passed the London interview and was accepted by the Royal Hong Kong Police as a Recruit Inspector.

On Friday, June 13th, 1975, I flew from Glasgow to London and thence to Hong Kong.

My parents were mortified.

Part 2

PTS [Police Training School]

I met four men on the London to Hong Kong flight who were to be my squad mates at the Police Training School (PTS) for eight months: Stewart from London, Ross from England via Singapore, Big Don from just outside Glasgow and Irish Mike who had served in the Royal Military Police in both Northern Ireland and Hong Kong.

Once we had gone through Hong Kong immigration and customs, we were met by affable, beer bellied Chief Inspector Keith Ratcliffe, who was wearing a greyish short-trousered safari suit with long grey socks and suede boots. It wasn't a good look, but Keith bought us all a beer. He said he was an instructor at PTS and escorted us to a police transit van which drove us from the airport to the School.

Soon as we got to PTS, a bunch of guys in uniform came over and ordered us to march to the parade ground in the gathering gloom. One uniformed shouter demanded to know why I'd turned up with shoulder length hair and bell bottoms to join the Royal Hong Kong Police. I didn't have a good answer so I kept my mouth shut. After being marched up and down the parade ground, we were ordered to stand at attention and the soft voiced padre came and whispered sweet nothings to us. We didn't complain, we'd been marching around in nearly 100% Hong Kong humidity for what seemed like forever.

Finally, we were marched towards some unlit buildings. We were commanded to halt and ordered to enter one of the buildings in single file. Suddenly, all the lights went on and a whole bunch of cheering, shouting, laughing guys came over and offered to buy us beers. It would have been churlish to refuse.

We'd just passed our initiation. We quickly learned the secret motto of the RHKP, "If you can't take a joke, you shouldn't have joined." We were introduced to Aussie Dave P and Kiwi, Graeme, as squadmates who'd arrived before us. After we had visited the two barracks which the seven of us would have as our home for the first nine weeks, we went to the infamous Wanchai red light area guided by our new pals. I visited bars open till the wee wee hours and ordered bottles of San Mig (San Miguel) from topless barmaids as I listened to Marty Robbins sing 'Big Iron' on the juke box. I began to think, 'know what? This ain't the Inner Temple, but I can handle it.'

San Mig was a Filipino beer. The Hong Kong transliteration was 'Saang Lik', meaning 'give birth to strength'. It always worked for me.

Our new found friends introduced us rapidly to Hong Kong as we went on a pub crawl, but made sure that we got back to our barracks by 3 am Hong Kong time (7 pm UK time).

The next day, being a Sunday, was a day off. Around 8 am, I went to the Officers Mess for breakfast. After a while Aussie Dave arrived, dressed in his customary checked shirt and slacks. He summoned the waiter and came out with the classic line, "Give us a f****ng beer mate!" I thought, *I really like this guy.* I'd heard there were people like this, but I'd never actually met one. We were friends from then on.

We spent the first week doing basic paperwork such as opening bank accounts and my shoulder length locks, were replaced by a very 'short back and sides'. We also got taken round Hong Kong for orientation. I got my first girlfriend, a 23-year-old Chinese ex-air hostess, from the squad ahead of us. She dumped me after a couple of dates. She wasn't pleased when I continued my karate practice after she'd come over to the gym on a spontaneous visit. Nope, May, still don't get it.

Incense Harbour

Hong Kong is crude romanisation of the Chinese term which means 'Incense Harbour', making incense was a major local industry. It is often mistranslated as 'Fragrant Harbour'.

After a series of 'unequal treaties', forced on China by British gunboat diplomacy, Hong Kong Island and the Kowloon Peninsula were ceded in perpetuity and the rural New Territories and around 400 islands were ceded until 1997 by China to the British Empire. Hong Kong was a colony acquired by Britain to facilitate the continuation (despite being contrary to Chinese law) of importing opium into China from India in return for tea, silk, gold and silver.

Bluntly, the Royal Navy was used to blow Chinese war junks and Guangdong province to kingdom come and force China to give up Chinese territory, including Hong Kong and to accept opium and all the concomitant evils that it brought in order to enrich British traders. To put it in context, imagine Chinese gunboats sailing up the Thames firing broadsides at the Houses of Parliament and forcing Her Majesty's government to cede the Isle of Wight and land from Portsmouth to Southampton to the Chinese, forcing us to accept Chinese opium in return for Scotch whisky and Bombay gin.

Hong Kong Chinese refer to all non-Chinese as *Gwailo* meaning demon fellow or *Gwai Mooi / Poh* meaning demon sister / wife

Good

There is an old Cantonese saying, 'Hong Kong, Good living, good eating.' For the prosperous few, this was true.

In 1975, the population was four million. Since then it has doubled due to both legal and illegal immigration from China. There has been a surge in pollution and construction too.

Hong Kong Island was the centre for government, administration, banking and business. There were some beautiful hills and the ultra-rich living on The Peak. There were also many housing estates and beautiful beaches.

The more Chinese commercial centre was the densely populated Kowloon Peninsula.

The New Territories were still quite rural in 1975, but now are covered by high-rise. The price of land is steep, so a lot of land has been reclaimed from the sea. Hong Kong also includes many islands, some populated, some not. The many harbours meant that smuggling to and from China of drugs, expensive cars and illegal immigrants is rife.

Hong Kong was divided into four police regions; Hong Kong Island, Kowloon, New Territories and Marine. Traditionally on Hong Kong Island police were referred to as 'police officers' , in Kowloon, police were referred to as 'cops', while in the New Territories, police were referred to as 'village guards'.

Language School

The seven expatriate officers in our squad included Big Don Logan, 6'4" and 230 pounds, moustachioed with red hair. He was immensely strong and skilled in ball games and field sports. He was the son of an ex Scots policeman and Commando war hero who had been engaged as a Force Training Officer at PTS. Don's family came from Paisley, just outside Glasgow. Don had attended school in Hong Kong and had worked for the Automobile Association. His great hero was big John Wayne.

Wiry, intense Stewart, 26, had been a store manager in Glasgow. He was from London. He had been in the army reserve.

Ross, a confident 19 year old of average build, was from England via Singapore. He was a keen rugby player.

Irish Mike, 24 who had matinee idol good looks, had served as in the Royal Military Police in both Northern Ireland and Hong Kong. Now, he wanted to be an officer. He had a secret Chinese family in Hong Kong. He was around 6'2" and 200 pounds.

Mike's room was just across the hall from mine. He gave me a copy of Camus' L'Etranger once. Most of the intro was underlined with red ink. He introduced me to Japanese food. He also taught me how to pour beer from a bottle into a glass. I gave him my old copy of 'the Good Soldier Svejk'. After reading a few chapters, he admitted finding the book funny, but said he couldn't continue with it as it was anti Catholic.

Kiwi was a college graduate. I found him somewhat miserly and mean spirited. He was just average. He eventually married a bar hostess.

Dave, the tall, gangly Aussie, was in his late 20s and had lived in Thailand for many years.

We started an eight-week intensive course in basic Cantonese, the most commonly spoken dialect in Hong Kong. The teachers were fine, but the material in our textbook was nothing like the street Cantonese we had started to pick up from the bars and hostelries. Fortunately, we all passed the language course. I managed to get a Credit. I could never get a Great Credit in Chinese because of my tone deafness (Chinese is a tonal language). I compensated by being more diligent and better in Chinese grammar and vocabulary.

Royal Hong Kong Police Recruit Inspector Squad 103 at Passing Out Dinner, February 1976. The author is 3rd from left.

Recruit Inspector Squad 103

After Language School, we acquired three Chinese squad mates, Norman, a Cantonese who had been promoted from police constable, 19 year old Rita, whose dad was a constable and Paul who had been promoted from Sergeant in the Airport Special Duties Unit. Paul's family was from Shandong in North East China. From then on we ten were collectively known as RI 103 (Recruit Inspector Squad 103).

The ten of us finally got individual rooms. I'd shared rooms with my brother, James, all my life, furthermore, our bedroom doubled as an admin room for my father. It was a great feeling to have my own private room at long last.

From Monday to Saturday, we had to attend morning roll call at 7 am in PT kit (shorts and plimsolls), we'd be in trouble if we weren't there. We would then have breakfast in the Officers Mess. After that, we would get into uniform (in summer, apart from Rita, we'd be bare-chested wear khaki shorts, black boots and a cap. In winter, we wore dark blue serge) and we marched everywhere. Fortunately, we had barrack room staff who cleaned our uniforms and polished our boots.

From the quiet time I'd had in Glasgow before and after graduation, I'd moved to one of the liveliest places in the world. I started looking for a martial arts school where I could get back into training. Through squad mate Paul, I started training at a Goju ryu (Hard / soft) karate school, and a Wing Chun school too – where I had some money stolen from my wallet. But the Goju-ryu wasn't what I wanted to do, while the Wing Chun uniform included a pair of long shorts which covered the knee joints. Not a good look.

I kept contact with home mainly by letter. One morning, I got mail from home. I was in tears as I read that my dear old boss, John Goodfellow, had died suddenly. He was a fine man, who taught me more about man-management than any psychologist could have done.

The food in the Officers Mess was fresh and tasty. There was also a very reasonably priced bar and a gym where I could practice my karate. If the weather was ok, we would sometimes go down to one of the nearby beaches for a swim or we might climb Brick Hill, which overlooked PTS. I spent almost all Saturday afternoons and Sundays as well as many evenings in town. The red light area of Wanchai was a good 30 minutes by taxi from PTS, a bus or PLB (public light bus) took a bit longer.

Recruit Inspector Docherty – Basic Training

Our RI 103 squad instructor was a genteel, fitness fanatic English Chief Inspector, Charlie Wimbush, who had served in Traffic, Marine and Anti-Corruption (by then the so called Independent Commission against Corruption had replaced the old Police Anti-Corruption Branch. In fact it wasn't independent, wasn't a commission and wasn't against corruption). Charlie was pleasant and fair-minded and a fitness fanatic who rowed competitively. He taught us law, police regulations and procedures, including how to take statements and reports, issuing traffic tickets and so on.

Our Drill and Musketry Instructor (DMI), was Senior Inspector Gus To, who liked to come across as a hard task masker, but who had a great sense of humour and was good at his job. We all liked him. The Chief Drill and Musketry Instructor (CDMI), was an ex British Army Sergeant Major. I didn't like him, so much so that whenever I was the squad prefect and we were marching around the Training School, if we passed him, I developed a coughing fit so that I didn't have to order the squad to do an 'Eyes right' or to salute him.

We learned to use 38 Colt Police Positive revolvers in all kinds of positions and at different ranges. We normally aimed at the body as that was the biggest target. We fired Remington pump action shotguns, gas pistols, wooden baton shell and gas guns, Sterling sub-machine guns and AR15 semi-automatic rifles. I'd never fired a proper gun before and quite enjoyed it, but though I am right handed, my left eye is much stronger. I was the worst shot in the squad. I went for additional shooting practice on Saturdays after duty, using .22 revolvers and automatic pistols. My shooting improved.

We were taught how to command a riot platoon, the RHKP had become world experts in this field. In1967, during the Chinese Cultural Revolution, there had been severe rioting in Hong Kong and the RHKP developed sophisticated riot training to deal with it.

As well as academic studies, we also had to train fitness, lifesaving and self-defence. Our squad's Physical Training Instructor (PTI) was a Sergeant called Peter. For the lifesaving training, we'd run along the scenic coastal roads from PTS to Deepwater Bay or Repulse Bay beaches and learn the techniques on the beach and in the South China Sea. We also learned how to paddle a kayak. It was a lot of fun and I was getting very well paid for it.

Fight?

People tell me I have an unfortunate manner. Big Don once said I could only ever go someplace twice. The second time was to apologise for the first time.

I could tell Stewart didn't like me. I'd never played basketball before. Stewart was very aggressive. He had his back to me and was cradling the ball so I slapped it out of his hands from behind. He immediately turned to bitch slap me. I saw it coming and hit him three times right between the eyes, causing concussion. Stewart wanted to continue, but I wasn't interested. Big Don said later that they were three of the fastest punches he had ever seen. Peter acted like nothing happened.

George Button

The CPTI (chief physical training instructor) at PTS, George Button, was a stocky Eurasian. He taught us police self-defence mainly based on Aikido (the way of harmonising energy) especially designed for control and restraint. He had excellent technique, but my squadmates found the moves difficult to apply. In my RI 103 squad of 10 recruits, I was the only one with a significant martial arts background.

I picked up the techniques more easily and George usually chose me to be his partner when demonstrating self-defence applications. I got on well with George and liked his stuff. George had been seconded to PTS from the Education Department. He was a civilian who taught self-defence to cops. He and his staff of police NCOs also trained us in gymnastics, athletics, ball games, life-saving and more. The problem was that six months wasn't enough time for George to impart the necessary self-defence skills to the average recruit. I found certain of George's moves to be somewhat on the tricky side.

I guess George had heard about the kid who trained karate on his own in the gym most evenings when classes were over for the day. One day, he came in and started to talk to me about martial arts in general. From then on, he was very friendly. He taught me field sports such as throwing the javelin, discus and shot putt. It was enormously interesting.

Squadmates

Stewart was a lot more pleasant company once his wife arrived in Hong Kong. After a few weeks, we made up.

Former police constable, Norman Ho, was wiry and above average height for a Cantonese. He told me that the difference between himself and Paul, the Shandong former sergeant. He said that if he was confronted by a high wall, he'd go over or around it, whereas Paul would try to smash his way through it.

Paul and Norman tried their best to win the Baton of Honour which was awarded to the top recruit inspector in each squad at the passing out parade. They were beaten to it by young super keen Ross who deserved the award. He served for a while in the Marine Police and later became a top Hong Kong Rugby administrator. He married a sweet English girl who had come out some years previously to visit her RHKP boyfriend.

Our attractive Chinese woman squad mate, Rita Chu, kept herself to herself, but was a nice person. She stayed with the RHKP all her working life.

Ross and Kiwi had been amazed at how cheap hi-fi systems were and even I finally bought one. I never owned a TV during my time in Hong Kong. I got into music and became a fan of Warren Zevon and Tom Waits.

So much for Miss Bowers.

Carry On Camping

While at PTS, we went on two camps with our instructor, Charlie Wimbush, camping was another new experience for me.

The first camp was just for the 10 members of RI 103 and consisted of one week in the dense undergrowth of the New Territories. We had to put up our own tents and build a fire. Charlie split us into groups and made us find places on our maps of the locality. We went orienteering and learned how to abseil. During one of the exercises, Big Don yelled, he'd been bitten on the leg by a snake. He even showed us the bite mark. We actually believed him and treated it as if real. It's not easy to lift someone the size of Big Don.

A couple of months later we went for another camp, this time with our constable squads. We did a couple of exercises where one squad posed as a group of illegal immigrants while another squad would try to locate and arrest them.

Charlie gave yours truly and N Squad the job of erecting the latrines, the wits in N Squad put up a big notice at the entrance on which was printed 'DOCHERTY'S CANTEEN'. What I didn't realise was at that time many Hong Kong Chinese had never used a Western style toilet so many recruit constables, instead of sitting on the toilet seats, they stood or squatted on them. At the end of the one-week camp of around 320 people, I was ordered to clean the latrines. To show a good example, I started to clean away the ordure on one of the toilet seats. N Squad reluctantly followed my lead.

Every night we socialised with our constables over some beer. With fellow Scot Big Don, I sang Billy Connolly's song, 'Last Train to Glasgow Central' and 'Old Macdonald had a Farm' (the unexpurgated version). Both camps were a lot of fun i.e. they were fun till bedtime, sleeping in those smelly canvas tents was no fun at all.

On Attachment

When we had been at PTS for six months, we were sent on attachment to different units for a few days. I was sent to EU / HKI (Emergency Unit Hong Kong Island), an eight hour shift responding to emergency calls in a patrol car with siren blaring and blue light flashing. Some weeks later, I was sent on attachment to Western Divisional Vice Squad. I was with a Shandong Station Sergeant. We did a couple of cases. It was strange to feel almost a police officer.

It was like dipping a toe into the water. We were not quite there yet.

Mess Nights

On mess nights, male officers wore white mess jackets, dark trousers with a stripe down each side, a white shirt and a black bow tie. Female officers wore black evening gowns. One of my new Chinese friends remarked to me that PTS Officers Mess was a goldfish bowl used by senior officers to observe the recruit inspectors.

Mess evenings involved a few beers in the downstairs bar then we'd go upstairs to the dining room for dinner seated at long tables with our squadmates. There would usually be at least a couple of RHKP bandsmen to play for us as we enjoyed our dinner, which was then followed by speeches, which the speaker would get up onto the table to deliver. There was always a Mess Night to farewell the senior squad before a passing out parade or to welcome a new squad.

After dinner, we'd saunter downstairs to the bar for Mess Games. We might start with a Boat Race. In this game, two teams of four guys (always guys) each from different squads, would face one another across a table. Each player would have a full pint of beer in front of him on the table. At a given signal, one man from each side would pick up his beer glass, skull the beer and put the empty beer glass back on the table in front of him. The first team to finish their four beers would be declared the winners. I was fourth fastest beer drinker in the squad so I just made the boat race team.

We also played jousting, where two male officers (again always guys), would get together as knight and steed and attempt to bump, push or pull the other horses and riders so that they fell to the ground. It was a case of last man standing. Big Don asked me if I wanted to give it a go. I immediately accepted as I had played the game many times during karate classes led by ex-paratrooper Al.

Not surprisingly, Big Don and I were a highly effective combination. The PTS Commandant, a cheerful bald Scotsman by name of MacNiven, sportingly took part one Mess Night. Big Don charged him and I grabbed him around the back of the neck and pulled. He went down rather heavily, as did one of the squad instructors, Tony Ferridge, who fractured his arm, "If you can't take a joke..."

One Mess Night just before the passing out parade, the senior squad representative, Phil T got up on the table to make a speech on behalf of the squad and proceeded to tell us how his squad was very upset that their Drill and Musketry Instructor had a falling out with the squad and had refused to attend the Mess Night.

I liked Phil and he had a point, but it left a sour taste. Shortly after we had made our way back down to the bar, I heard a ruckus upstairs and found out that the Chief Drill and Musketry Instructor had hit Phil full in the face with his beer glass. A clear case of wounding with intent. We are talking prison time. Amazingly, it was all swept under the carpet, but from then on, Phil and his squad mates refused to salute the CDMI up to and including the passing out parade.

Tai Chi Master

George Button had trained in the Chinese martial arts. After I had known George for a couple of months, I confided in him that I wanted to learn Tai Chi, he told me about his Tai Chi master, a Sifu (teaching father) named Cheng Tin-hung, the best fighting Tai Chi instructor in South East Asia.

I went with Paul, my squadmate, to the bustling Mongkok district in Kowloon to visit George's old Tai Chi Sifu. We took the lift up to the 11th floor of a grimy apartment block and entered a room with a sign hanging outside, which read, Cheng Tin-hung Tai Chi Institute. Paul introduced us to a broad-shouldered Cheng, who was around 45 years old. He was of slightly more than average height for a Cantonese male of his time, but had a stocky build with powerful back and shoulder muscles. He had a big belly, was unshaven, wearing shorts, flip-flops and a string vest. A cigarette dangled from his lips. I learned that he smoked five packs a day. He never seemed to finish a cigarette he'd light up, take a couple of puffs then stub it out. I could see he had many scars all around his body. He later told me that in his youth he had been in a number of knife fights.

Cheng had fond memories of his old student 'George Pak' as he called George Button and after showing us many international Chinese full contact trophies and medals displayed around the studio, he took us up to the rooftop. Around 40 guys and a couple of ladies, some in groups, some in pairs, some singly, were practicing Tai Chi forms, weapons and applications.

They were highly respectful to Cheng and all addressed Cheng as 'Sifu'.

With the cigarette still in his mouth, Cheng called over a couple of male students and proceeded to throw them around with ease. He then mentioned Tai Chi Nei Kung (internal strength) and asked me to punch him to the body. When I did karate sparring, I was able to knock people down with body shots. Cheng took my best punches with ease. I had found my master. From that day on, I have never trained with anyone else and regarded Cheng as my Sifu until his death in 2005.

The class ended and when I came back the next evening, Cheng told me that George had come to try him out some years previously and though he had only trained in Tai Chi self-defence for about six months, he had no trouble in mastering the techniques. He said he would hide nothing from me, because as a non-Chinese, no one would want to learn from me, so I was no threat to him.

When next I met George, I told him everything and thanked him profusely. He was delighted and told me a few stories about Cheng applying techniques on various people. From time to time, George would ask me how things were going. I'll always be grateful for what this fine man did for me, a raw recruit.

Operational Orders

One of the most interesting and useful things that I learned in PTS was how to write operational orders.

We were taught the mantra, "Failing to plan is planning to fail."

Operational orders are a format for dealing with major events used by police and military.

The main headings are:

SITUATION – RHKP INSPECTOR. MALE. AGED 21. SINGLE. SAVINGS IN BANK.

MISSION – TO BECOME TAI CHI SIFU

EXECUTION – LEARN COMPLETE ART IN HONG KONG FROM SIFU CHENG. BE SUCCESSFUL IN CHINESE FULL CONTACT. IMPROVE KNOWLEDGE OF CHINESE LANGUAGE AND CULTURE. LEARN TO WRITE BETTER.

It was all a long time ago, but a lot of what I learned has proven useful in civilian life.

Probationary Inspector Docherty – School's Out

After two intensive months of language school and six months of law, police regulations and procedures, drill, musketry, fitness training, self-defence, etc. I was ready for the passing out parade. Each member of Recruit Inspector Squad 103 was allowed to invite two guests to attend the passing out parade and reception afterwards in the Officers Mess. Somewhat to the dismay of my squad instructor, Charlie, I invited cynical 'any place where it's warm.' Dave, who had served in the Royal Canadian Mounted Police Surveillance Unit and a Kiwi called Ski, both of whom had failed language school and were working out their three-month's notice doing admin. I am still friends with Dave.

Before our passing out, we had to conduct the traditional initiation on the new arrivals. I was introduced as 'Father Docherty', PTS padre. The new guys were taken in – just as we had been.

On the morning of the parade, each of us recruit inspectors in turn had to march our police constable squads (my squad was N Squad) onto the parade ground to the stirring sound of the Royal Hong Kong Police Band playing 'Scotland the Brave'.

The inspecting officer was a kindly old gent of Portuguese extraction whose family had been involved in the China trade and he was now one of the 'great and the good' in Hong Kong Society. We stood at attention in front of our squads as he inspected us in turn. We were in so-called winter uniform, a blue serge ensemble with black patent leather soled shoes and a peaked cap with Royal Hong Kong Police badge and the classic black leather Sam Browne belt and cross strap. We looked damn good.

The last time I saw George was just a few days before the passing out. I heard George was proud of me as Gus To was when I finally became a champion.

Inspector Docherty
The Northern Lights
of Old Aberdeen

I was posted to a place the Chinese called Heung Kong Jai (literally 'Little Incense Harbour'). In English, it was called Aberdeen. Ironically, the boundary of Aberdeen police sub-division started right outside PTS. Aberdeen Police Station was five minutes' walk from PTS.

Aberdeen Sub-Divisional Inspector (SDI) was highly experienced Chief Inspector, Steve Tang. I was put in charge of a sub-unit of about 30 constables and five sergeants. My two I / C (Second in Command) was a huge Station Sergeant, Mr Keung. I saw him crying once when he was telling me about the family he had lost in Shandong when the Communists took over. He was a good man, brave, honest and 100% reliable.

There were two other Station Sergeants from Shandong at Aberdeen and many more in other divisions. The majority of constables and NCOs were Hong Kong Cantonese. The Shandong thought of themselves as being hard-working, loyal and direct, but were considered unsophisticated, physically intimidating and not very bright by the local Cantonese. The Cantonese thought of themselves as much smarter than anyone else including expatriate officers like me. The Shandong considered the Cantonese sly and tricky. There was some truth in all these points of view.

I was given a lot of admin to do, mainly death reports. Kids from families living on junks moored in the harbour would disappear, presumably drowned. One time I had to investigate a case where the deceased was found dead in his own home with an electric wire tied around his penis. The other end of the flex was plugged in and switched on. Whether it was an attempt at sexual gratification or a suicide, I'll never know.

Aberdeen was an unusual place. There were four huge housing estates in the sub-division and Tai Chi master Cheng's brother lived in one of them. Occasionally, we'd meet up for 'Yam cha'. This is Cantonese for 'Drink Tea' but basically meant going to a restaurant anytime between 6 am to 3 pm for a drink of tea / beer/ Cognac and some snacks.

Why the Chinese preference for cognac over whisky? Apparently, those sneaky Frenchies had told the priapic Chinese that, 'Whisky makes you 6.30, brandy makes you 12 o'clock.'

Other main areas in Aberdeen were the harbour and Aplichau Island. The harbour was largely the responsibility of the Marine Police. Aplichau was a den of iniquity for drugs and illegal casinos and in those days, we needed to hire a sampan to cross over to the island to do drugs and gambling raids.

Aberdeen sub-division also included the beaches at Repulse Bay and Deepwater Bay and some very expensive properties. On one occasion, I had to visit Sir Stanley Ho for the annual firearms Inspection. He offered me an aperitif which I accepted. Though a casino billionaire, he was affable and very pleasant.

Another time, I was put in charge of a team from Aberdeen Police Station to provide security at the Repulse Bay Hotel where the 1976 Miss Universe contestants were staying. Later that week, on one of my days off, I had to go with Sifu Cheng and fellow students to the theatre where the Miss Universe Contest was being staged and do a short routine of Tai Chi wrestling techniques with Tai Chi elder brother, Tong Chi-kin, to the tune of 'Everybody Loves Kung Fu Fighting'.

Wilson

Aberdeen was part of Western Division, Divisional Superintendent, John Wilson, was an intelligent, humorous fellow. Gambling authorisations required the signature of a superintendent or above. Rather than disturb him, he told me to do any raids I needed to and he would sign the authorisation afterwards. This worked fine until late one night I raided an illegal casino and arrested around 20 people. When I went back to work the next day, intending to call Wilson, I bumped into Steve Tang. He told me, "The boss has been arrested by ICAC."

I was somewhat unnerved by this, unless I got a gambling authorisation from the Assistant Divisional Superintendent (ADS), I would be guilty of kidnapping. Fortunately, for the first time, the ADS issued a post facto authorisation and I was able to process the case.

I liked and respected John Wilson, but had heard that his mistress had opened an unlicensed massage parlour in Western Division and Wilson had been the guest of honour at the opening ceremony. It turned out that the ICAC had arrested him for corruption in respect of his previous posting. He was convicted and was given seven years. Wilson was a dinosaur, he couldn't adjust to the new RHKP and paid the price.

Knife Maniac

One time, I was in the patrol car with a big highly experienced constable when we got a call about a knife incident. Siren blaring and blue light flashing, off we went to the premises, a domestic flat. We got there to find a mentally ill teenager threatening his family with a six-inch blade.

The constable and I were both carrying .38 Colt revolvers, but my experienced companion had taken the precaution of equipping himself with a rattan shield and a long baton from the back of the patrol car. The boy was wielding the knife behind a dining table. In a classic pincer movement, I went left round the table, my companion went right.

The knife boy lurched to his left, knife at the ready. My PC driver in one moment let go his long baton and brought his rattan shield down on the knife arm, trapping it on the table and coolly took the knife away from the troubled teen.

Guns are dangerous. They should be a last resort.

Police Casino

One of the files I had concerned a premises which, was suspected of being used as an illegal casino. One afternoon, I did a surprise raid only to find more than 20 members of a sub-unit from Aberdeen Police Station playing cards at a big table. There was no money on the table.

I looked at the senior sergeant and he looked at me.

No one said anything.

When I got back to my office, I wrote details of the raid, noting that no suspicious activities were detected. I didn't want to know anymore. The truth is what gets reported. Right?

Justice

At about 2 am one night shift, a taxi driver reported that he'd taken an expat male fare all the way from the airport to Repulse Bay only for the passenger to refuse to pay and instead to lock himself inside his flat. On my arrival, I banged on the front door and shouted to him to open up and said if he didn't do so, I would kick down the door.

He didn't open up so I kicked open the door to reveal an English guy in his 30s. We managed to get him to pay, but he later made a complaint against me, so I had to go see Irish District Commander, Porky Grace, who said my sense of justice was commendable but I had been overly enthusiastic.

TAI CHI Training

Despite the fact that a round trip from Aberdeen, where I was living and working to Mongkok to see Sifu Cheng, took almost two hours, I kept up my training even when on shift work.

Sometimes, I attended morning Tai Chi sessions from 10 am till noon, sometimes evening sessions from 8 pm till 10 pm. These were 'class times', but during many a class time, Sifu would spend all or most of the time downstairs in his studio, playing mahjong or watching TV. Even when he did come up to the rooftop, he'd often just walk around smoking a cigarette, deep in thought. Occasionally, he'd explain a technique or application. Sometimes he'd join in the training himself, especially Tai Chi wrestling and free pushing hands. Mostly, he delegated the basic training to a senior student. Often, there were half a dozen pairs and several small groups all practicing different things.

After a few months, Sifu said that I could come anytime.

True to Form

Sifu Cheng started me off by appointing a senior student to show me 'Square Long Form' where the movements were like block letters, the postures were precise, but there was no flow or continuity of movement. There were more than 500 movements, more than 40 different techniques, some repeated many times. It took me nearly four months to learn the Long Form square and round. Square Form had been invented by Wu Jianquan (teacher of Sifu's uncle, Cheng Wing-kwong) in the 1930s when teaching large groups of students at Beijing University. There is usually a feeling of completion on the count of three and the moves are made to fit this count.

After mastering Square Form, we moved onto the Round Form which was much more complex involving a lot of coiling and twisting.

Square Form gives a clear structure to techniques, but it involves a dumbing down and many practitioners end up doing form which is neither square nor round. There is also a Mirror Form where left becomes right and vice versa and Reverse Form, which starts at the finish and ends at the beginning. Hand Form is complex as indeed, are all the weapon forms, all require 'decoding'.

Sifu Cheng told me that Qi Minxuan, his mysterious North China master, would sometimes do the Hand Form in such a way that he could not follow.

Snap

This is all reminiscent of Chinese calligraphy, where there are six methods. The most complex is called 'Grass' which even skilled calligraphers find difficult to read. Like martial arts, it's all about expressing concepts through technique. Only in martial arts, not everyone is able to maintain good technique under pressure.

In my decades of practicing forms and decoding the individual movements, I have operated on the premises that;

Everything is something – all the moves have meaning (or had).

The likeliest explanation is the usually the correct one (Occam's razor).

Each turn represents a new opponent / new situation.

The lack of head turns in Tai Chi forms is to develop peripheral vision so we can deal with multiple opponents coming from different angles.

Not all attacks or defences are made face to face with an opponent.

Many techniques are designed for using against two / more opponents.

Many techniques are designed as follow-ups to the previous technique.

A step can be a kick.

What you practice is what you will use.

I was meticulous in taking notes.

Applications

Sifu was delighted to see that I was good at martial applications, which he started showing me from the first session. He said that I had a good physique. In my nine years in Hong Kong, I went to Sifu Cheng's rooftop most days.

Sifu Cheng described quite a few techniques and postures as linkage. I found it hard to believe that the ancient masters of the martial art that is Tai Chi needed to include meaningless linkage. I found him to be a tiger rather than a dragon. He advocated shouting, swearing and spitting at opponents. Just not me and inappropriate for a police officer.

I prefer to be the 'one strike kill silent assassin'.

There was no mention of Nei Kung. Yet.

I once spent two hours with a senior practicing basic Four Directions pushing hands. Sifu Cheng had probably just forgotten about us. The teaching standard and skill of the senior students varied considerably, I always checked everything that I was told or shown by the seniors with Sifu Cheng.

Compared to what I was used to in karate, there was no structure to the training. The belt and grading system of Japanese martial arts has its critics, but one big advantage is that students can feel that they have a target to aim for and the syllabus is taught in a coherent way with a feeling of progression from simpler moves and forms to much more complex ones. Apart from the Square Form, very little Tai Chi material was broken down and made easier to learn. It quickly became clear to me that though the Square Form was easier to learn, it had moves that were ludicrous from a martial point of view.

As I came to know Sifu better, he'd often ask me to have meals with him, sometimes in his apartment with the family, sometimes in a restaurant. This was usually a good time for asking questions. My Cantonese was improving too, so I got a lot more out of these informal sessions.

After training in the morning sessions, some of us would accompany Sifu to 'yam cha' drink(tea) in the nearby Million Golden Dragons Restaurant and there he would have his personal bottle of cognac from which he'd invite us to have a snifter.

In the late evenings, after classes finished at 10 pm, we'd go to a Malaysian restaurant for curry and beer. Sifu tended to prefer a soft drink with white bread toast with evaporated milk and sugar poured over it. Over the years his diabetes symptoms got worse, he got more tired, more quickly as well as having problems with balance.

Tiger Dragon Phoenix

There is a Chinese saying, "Eat anything that flies except a helicopter, anything that swims except a submarine and anything with four legs except a table."

Aussie Dave had been posted to Shataukok Police Station up near the Hong Kong China Border. I went up to see him for a couple of days.

Just after my arrival, a police Landrover entered the station compound and a little old Chinese guy got out. In one hand, he held a big sack, in the other hand he was carrying a dead wildcat. He put down the dead cat and emptied the contents of the sack onto the ground. I've never seen cops move so fast when they saw a 9' long brown python come tumbling out of the sack, angrily spitting and hissing.

The little old Chinese guy armed only with the sack and some special liquid he sipped and then spat at the snake's head. He re-captured the python very easily. He was a professional snake catcher. He told us he would sell the wildcat and snake to a local restaurant which made an aphrodisiac dish called Tiger, Dragon, Phoenix. The cat would represent the tiger, the snake was the dragon and wild fowl was the phoenix.

Over the years, I tried many exotic dishes. As in life, so with food, there have to be lines. In my own case, I'll eat deer nether regions but only dog stew, not its organs. Tricky.

1976 – Nei Kung public demo. A fellow student jumps on author's
abdomen from shoulder height.

Nei Kung

After I'd been training with him for about five months, Sifu Cheng asked me if I was interested in learning Tai Chi 24 exercise Nei Kung. I told him that I was.

I'd noticed that during training hours, some advanced students would go down to Sifu Cheng's studio. I realised that they were receiving special training, but decided to be patient.

Before learning the Nei Kung, I went through a ritual ceremony of discipleship called 'Baishi'. There was an additional fee for Nei Kung.

'Bai' means to worship or to pay respects, 'Shi' is the teaching / the teacher. Daniel Chan, one of the seniors, translated the 12 regulations concerning Nei Kung. I had to offer three incense sticks to show respect to the memory of the founder and to bow to Sifu Cheng and then to any elder brothers present.

After this, I was considered to be a Disciple / Door Person rather than a mere student and had access to being taught 'Inside the Door' techniques. This was mainly an oral tradition. Some hidden / inside the door techniques existed in the forms, but the names couldn't be found in any book. Their names were taught orally only. There are also definite techniques in the forms with applications, but without any names. More 'linkage' Sifu?

Sifu Cheng showed me the 12 Yin Nei Kung exercises first. Each time I did the exercises, my body shook uncontrollably. This went on for a few weeks, but then I got used to them. Some of the static exercises were meditative and highly effective in strengthening the joints and improving circulation. The moving exercises had health benefits as well as applications. After 100 days of no sex and practicing the exercises almost every day, Sifu Cheng tested me by getting one of the seniors to jump on my abdomen from shoulder height. No problem.

Shortly after this, he taught me the 12 Yang exercises which were more dynamic and physically demanding than the 12 Yin. This was exactly the kind of material I wished to understand and eventually teach.

Show Off

I was in Western Officers Mess having a beer with Lawrence, Nigel, Jesus and others when someone asked what had I learned in my Kung Fu practice. I told them about the Nei Kung, how I could take punches, kicks and jumps.

This the guys wanted to see, especially the jumps. So after taking their best shots, I lay on the floor and one by one, they climbed onto the bar and jumped on my abdomen. The guys were amazed.

Funny, none of them wanted to try it.

Karmic Connection?

Unlike many, Sifu Cheng Tin-hung never misled students. He'd either teach you or he wouldn't. He didn't treat us all the same, because in his eyes we were not the same. It was a matter of karmic connection. I guess for a long while we both felt we had a special connection right from the start.

Unlike many Hong Kong Kung Fu Sifu, he had nothing to do with Black Societies (triad gangs), indeed, he had taught many police officers over the years.

He drank sparingly, and I only saw him the worse for wear twice. The first time was after drinking Russian vodka. The second time was after we had been eating Mexican food and drinking tequila. Both times, he went straight to bed.

Apart from mahjong, he didn't gamble. He'd tried opium a few times and had smoked heroin once. Just for the experience. He said it was amazing and that he now understood why people take it.

Regarding money, Sifu's attitude was that it was for spending –especially if it belonged to someone else. I was aware of this penchant of his and each Chinese New Year, I'd give him a $1000 Hong Kong gold coin.

Sifu often showed me partnered drills and their practical application in training distance, timing and angle when dealing with the opponent. Once I could do it, he'd pass me to a senior. Drills included:

Seven Stars Step, Four Corner Step and Nine Palace Step which trained sidestepping and spinning.

Flying Flower Palm, Five Element Arm, Running Thunder Hand, Using the Forearm to Force the Door. All trained entry and striking.

Gyrating Arms, Retreat then Advance, Reeling Silk. Six Secret Words, The Uprooting Wave were all concepts expressed in application. Sifu's point of view was that Tai Chi's martial aspects should only be taught to those who could use them effectively. He was at his best when he talked of fighting. He had plenty of experience.

He went to Taiwan in 1957 as a member of the Hong Kong Chinese full contact team. He was the only one to win against the Taiwanese, he defeated the Taiwan middleweight champion. He was introduced to the famous painting and Tai Chi master, Cheng Man-ching, who gave Sifu one of his paintings. He said that Cheng Man-ching was very soft in pushing hands, but that was all.

Some of Sifu's stuff reminded me of Nanbu. He rarely hit people and had excellent control, but like my father, he had a ferocious temper and used plenty of invective.

The Book

In 1976, Sifu told me that he intended to publish a new book, The Chinese title meant TCC Narration of Requirements, I translated it as 'Transcendent Art'. What did you expect? I was only 22.

He said that he wanted me to rewrite a few pages that had been translated into English and he required me to be in a few photos. I did the translation and appeared in more than 50 photos, mainly self-defence applications and spear. This was massive recognition. I was in more photos than anyone else even though I'd only been training with him for a year and was wearing flared or bell bottom trousers at the time. The book is still in print.

He got me doing public demos. My specialities were Nei Kung (taking someone jumping on my abdomen from head height or having two guys simultaneously kick me with jump and roundhouse kicks), Tai Chi self-defence and wrestling, and spear form, never Hand Form.

He also got me to join the Committee of the Hong Kong Chinese Martial Arts Association. I was the only non-Chinese member. Occasionally, my legal background and English language skills came in useful, so I accompanied Sifu to all the meetings.

For some reason, he seemed to trust me. Not quite that simple.

Sport and Recreation

In 1976, the Hong Kong Government Sport and Recreation Department did something brave and dramatic that changed the lives of a huge number of people. They approached Sifu Cheng and asked him, as Hong Kong's best-known Tai Chi master, to send his senior students to open free Tai Chi classes in some of the poorest public housing estates in Hong Kong to improve the health and wellbeing of residents. It was a phenomenal success.

Students of the new classes in the housing estates embarked on a programme of training for about three months practicing square hand form followed by another three months of round hand form. People did six months, then what?

Sifu opened Tai Chi teacher training courses for the graduates. Sometimes, there were more than 70 people in a class. Most of them were female and over 40 years of age. Very quickly people like me, who trained Tai Chi as a martial art, were in the minority. More and more people knew less and less. The quality and quantity of training partners at Sifu Cheng's school became much lower. Sifu's senior students became too busy with the new classes. On the plus side, the classes improved public health and well-being. The teachers and Sifu made some money.

Family Visits

After I'd been in the RHKP for just over a year, my parents flew out to Hong Kong to visit me for a week. They found it interesting, especially my father. They had one contact from Glasgow, Stuart Waldman, from the City of Glasgow Police, who had joined the Independent Commission against Corruption (ICAC) as a senior officer. I liked him, but realised that we could not be friends.

My parents were not at all happy that I didn't go to church anymore. We didn't really get on.

In 1977, my late brother James came to stay with me for a couple of weeks. I think he enjoyed the food and the shopping, but Hong Kong didn't really suit his quiet temperament.

My late brother Charlie also visited just before he became a police officer himself in North Yorkshire. I remember squad mate, Mike M, trying to get hold of us by phone when we were enjoying a beer in the Red Lips bar, only to be told, "There's just a couple of kids here having a beer."

I was 27 at the time.

My karate black belt brother, Andy, came over too when he was at Liverpool University, waiting to join the army. He wound up in Military Intelligence, an Arabic speaker, specialising in the Middle East. I played a few tricks on him, like introducing him to Szechuan chillies, to prepare this fine young person for the vicissitudes of military life.

Tong Chik-Tak – The Challenge

Granda Docherty once said, "Some folks are champ dancers, others are damned chancers."

Sifu Cheng, was something of a damned chancer. I went to a few dance halls with him, but he only ever watched.

One day in the summer of 1976, just after the fight between Muhammad Ali and the Japanese wrestler Inoki, I visited Sifu's studio only to find him giving a press conference, at which he announced that his Scottish student, Police Inspector Tong Chik-tak (my official Chinese name) was challenging Muhammad Ali to a fight in Hong Kong, Tai Chi against Western Boxing.

Naturally, Sifu hadn't consulted me at all.

The Hong Kong gutter press loved this kind of 'fake news' and were only too happy to publish Sifu's bullshit. You had to admire the effrontery of the man. Ali's people didn't reply. It was a win-win for Sifu.

A few months later in late July 1976, Sifu Cheng asked me if I was interested in representing the school in Chinese full contact competition.

At that time, there was only one Chinese full contact fighter in the school, Chow Kim-tong, a short and stocky middleweight. Chow also practiced Western Boxing and told me that he hoped to become an Olympic champion boxer. Chow was very fit and was hard as nails. This was what I had come to Hong Kong for. I knew that the best way to succeed with my plan to become a credible professional Tai Chi instructor was to win in Chinese full contact competition against other styles.

Scattering Hands Platform

Scattering Hands Platform is the literal translation of San Shou Leitai and this is how Chinese martial artists traditionally fought full contact. Normally in Hong Kong, the full contact platform was around two feet in height and around 24 feet x 24 feet in dimension. Unlike a boxing ring, there were no ropes. Fighters could use hand, elbow, foot, knee and shoulder strikes, locks, trips, sweeps and throws. Normally only the groin was not a target.

The fact that the platform was raised and that there were no ropes made it very dangerous to be thrown from the platform. Often, I witnessed broken legs and arms as a result. It was what I had to do to achieve my goal.

I was told by Sifu Cheng that the full contact competition would take place in three months' time. For the next three months, I practiced Nei Kung and hand form every day.

Then Sifu added, "No girls no alcohol."

Five days a week, I practiced Handstands.

20 minutes punching with a lead weight of over four pounds in each hand doing 150 Running Thunder Hand strikes per minute. Totally 3000 punches in 20 minutes.

3 x 2 minutes rounds of forward rolls – at least 80 rolls per round.

3 x 2 minutes rounds of striking a heavy bag.

3 x 2 minutes of taking conditioning blows to the head, body and legs at about half strength.

3 x 3 minutes rounds of Running Thunder Hand on focus pads.

Tai Chi Wrestling. Sifu, partly because of his stocky build, was an excellent wrestler, particularly skilled in grappling and locking techniques. He had picked up a few ideas from Judo practitioners when he had spent six months teaching Tai Chi in Japan. Throwing techniques earned big points in full contact and were highly effective against punchers and kickers.

Full Contact Sparring.

It was quite a commitment.

The author celebrating after knocking out the Chinese Full Contact Champion of Hong Kong in 1976.

Full Contact

The competition was held at a Sports Hall in Wanchai. I had been coerced by John Wilson into drinking half a bottle of ginseng brandy, the night before my first big test at a dinner in Aberdeen. All Western Division inspectors and above had been ordered to attend by John Wilson to give 'face' to the kaifong (local representatives). I, then, was working in Aberdeen most of the day of the fight, so I was late getting to the stadium. I found out afterwards that Sifu had been going round telling his Chinese students that I was afraid and would not come.

Nice.

When the time of my fight came, I looked around the packed stadium full of Hong Kong Chinese shouting and gesticulating at me. I felt somewhat lonesome till I spotted my PTS chums who had come to support me, led by Dave Inglis and John Heptonstall. I was a Scottish Police Inspector from a Tai Chi school going to fight Chinese full contact against the top local heavyweight Choy Li Fut guy who was also Hong Kong Judo Champ. No problem.

All fighters were dressed in either red or blue chest protectors, T-shirts and shorts, groin protectors, head protectors and 4 oz gloves. I was dressed in red, my favourite colour.

It ended in the 3rd round. His corner threw in the towel.

I don't remember too much about it except he started with a headshot which didn't hurt. I do remember hitting him with uppercuts (which we'd never done in training) and I caught his legs every time he tried to kick me, but he had long arms and sometimes he managed to follow up with a head shot.

The lads from PTS were a fantastic support. A foreign legion of Anglos, Celts, Kiwis, Aussies, Canadians and Chinese. I felt I owed them big time. It turned out I didn't need to pay for beer in PTS Officers Mess for a month afterwards.

Mr Shum

One day I was talking to Sifu about Qigong (working with breath and energy). Sifu told me about a Tai Chi elder brother of mine, Mr Shum, a slight, intense businessman.

Shum's wife had dragged her husband to Sifu's place. She told Sifu that Shum was ejaculating spontaneously at all hours and he felt his Qi energy was locked in his chest and wouldn't go up or down, it made him feel he could fly.

Sifu said that elder brother Shum had definitely been practicing sexual Qigong (also known as Nei Dan / Internal Alchemy) and he was practicing something that was inherently dangerous or practicing wrongly and so the autonomic nervous system was suffering side effects. This was called 'walk fire enter demon.' The only way was to take Shum's attention away from his Qi.

Sifu called some of his young male students to come over and told them to practice free push hands with Shum (Tai Chi training trying to keep your own balance while trying to unbalance an opponent) with Shum. After a couple of hours Shum fell asleep, totally exhausted. Every time Shum woke up, it was more push hands. It took three days to cure him.

Even then, he had to go back home with his ever loving wife to explain why the sexual Qigong.

Esoteric Practices

Certain Chinese martial arts schools practice Shenda (Spirit Boxing), I saw Chinese police officers practice it. Sifu condemned it as highly dangerous as the boxers would go into a trance and invoke spirits such as famous warrior Chang Fei or even the Monkey King – a fictional character (from the novel Journey to the West) to possess them. They would then strike their torsos with bladed weapons without harming themselves.

During the Boxer Rebellion in 1900, the secret society of Righteous and Harmonious Fists even believed that they were impervious to bullets until General Yuan Shi-kai, Governor of Shandong Province, tested them with Lee Enfield rifles with predictable results.

One of the constables in Aberdeen showed me a sacred red sash his Sifu had given him which made him invulnerable to blades and bullets. He wore it under his uniform. For real.

Cheng Tin-hung had no time for such nonsense.

Sifu Cheng learned Xian Jia Baduanjin (Immortal Family eight Pieces of Brocade), an Internal Alchemy Qigong system from his uncle, who had learned it from an itinerant Taoist. Sifu was conservative in sexual matters, I was only the third person he taught it to.

Sifu's uncle had concubines and was an itinerant businessman, so I guess he felt the need to learn Internal Alchemy to keep the ladies happy.

Sifu Cheng took a dim view of sexual activity of any kind, unless for procreation.

Sifu had firm views on a variety of subjects He became interested in Feng Shui (literally 'Wind and Water'). This was the science of geomancy. Everything in harmony and in its proper place.

Sifu was an obsessive and prone to bursts of enthusiasm. He started to collect stamps. He then became a collector of ancient Chinese coins rescued from ancient tombs on his land in China.

He later took to hill walking every Sunday. Some of us students would sleep in his studio overnight. We'd get up before 6 am, go for dim sum then take a train or bus to the New Territories or one of the many islands. Invariably, he wore a Sherlock Holmes style deerstalker hat, short trousers and he held a cane.

We would sometimes walk ahead pretending we weren't with him.

He next bought a large tent and started the trips on the Saturday. Invariably, he'd wake everyone up around 4 am, explaining he was afraid, we were thirsty. He'd then produce a bottle of cognac. The truth was, he himself couldn't sleep and he wanted someone to talk to.

Sifu Cheng Philosophy

Sifu Cheng was married three times. I never met his first wife, who was said to be ferocious. His second wife was from the same village as Sifu. She was pleasant and was a full time wife and mother, but also taught Nei Kung to pregnant ladies. His third wife was also from the village and had worked in the restaurant. She was 40 years younger than Sifu.

He got rid of wife two by paying off local officials to remove the registration of his marriage to her. As there was no record of their marriage, there was no need to get a divorce and he was free to marry again.

Sifu on women, "woman is the enemy of the hero."

"In the whole world, there is no good woman, except for your mother."

He told me that when he'd spent six months teaching in Japan, he had sex with as many Japanese girls as possible in revenge for what the Japanese did to the Chinese during the war.

When he went to a nightclub, Sifu Cheng liked to see other guys in the group having fun with the hostesses. I believe it is called voyeurism.

Singapore Sling

My full contact triumph in Wanchai, got me selected to represent Hong Kong in the Fourth South East Asian Chinese Full Contact Championships in December 1976. My sobriquet in the Hong Kong kung fu world was 'Ah Dan' / (Cinnabar).

I'd heard a few things about Singapore from my old karate friend, 'Chalky' Whitehouse, who loved practicing nunchaku, but who was so bad at it, he had to wear a motorcycle helmet to protect his head. He had great stories like when he visited Singapore and found out the hard way how you can take the lady boy out of Bugis Street but if you want more, it's always better not to use Barclaycard.

I visited Bugis Street with Cheng Tin hung and other members of the Hong Kong Kung Fu team in 1976 when we were in Singapore for the Fourth SE Asian Chinese Full Contact Championships. It was hot and humid. After no sex or alcohol for 100 days, the 'girls' began to look strangely attractive…

When I was last in Singapore back in 2000 or so, I met up with TCC cousin and old chum, Michael Ngiam. The Raffles Hotel is still there full of freemasons drinking Singapore Gin Slings, but Bugis Street is now an air-conditioned shopping mall and metro station. It ain't hot no more. Most of the lady boys have had the operation by now.

Back in 1976, when we got to the hotel room in Singapore, Sifu Cheng handed me a small brown medicine bottle. The label read, 'Anabolic Steroids'. I refused to take them. I may be naive, but I wanted to beat my opponents with Tai Chi, not with drugs. Sifu Cheng was a piece of work.

Our lines were drawn in different places.

I met students of my teacher's uncle at the Championships. They had plenty to say about how good the uncle was, but I noticed none of them had any students fighting in the competition. However, they did everything they could to support us. Sifu Chau from Singapore had a herbalist shop and was particularly generous, supplying Chow Kim-tong and me with highly expensive raw ginseng to eat before each fight and papaya afterwards to bring us down

The fighters wore chest and groin protectors with very thin gloves – almost like driving gloves with the tops cut off the finger protection. We were not allowed to hit repeatedly to the head, but many folk did. I did not.

In those days, I was heavily influenced by Confucius and Legalist philosophers, especially Han Feizi, and their concepts of correct behaviour, crime and fitting punishment. I wonder why. I taught it to my kids by putting them both into martial arts when they were three years old.

No need to thank me Junior.

The author with Sifu Cheng Tin-hung and Chow Tim-tong with his Heavyweight Division 2nd place Merlion trophy at the 4th South East Asian Chinese Full Contact Championships in Singapore in 1976.

If You Can't Take The Punches...

My first opponent was Malaysian from Chikechuan style, a blend of Thai Boxing, Western Boxing and Choy Li Fut (itself a blend of three styles). He was considerably heavier and considerably shorter than me. He was good in sweeping and, attacking the legs and feet with low kicks and stamps, following up with heavy headshots.

I threw him with Tai Chi wrestling technique Double Hands Seize Legs when he tried a Choy Li Fut swing punch to the head. This was one of Sifu's Inside the Door' techniques. The name can't be found in any Tai Chi book. You duck under a punch to the head and seize the opponent behind both knees, simultaneously barging him in the abdomen.

I also threw him off the high fighting platform half a dozen times. He had nothing left so his corner threw in the towel.

I'd won the fight, but I was badly injured with another fight coming up in three days' time. I had two black eyes, a bleeding nose, cut lips and heavy bruising on my left leg and foot, so bad that I couldn't put a shoe on my left foot.

I was taken by Sifu Cheng to see the team doctor, a herbalist who got me to swallow bear gall bladder and wear a herbal mudpack on the damaged foot and leg. After three days of this treatment, I was ready to fight again. I was in pain every time I moved.

My next fight was against a Shaolin fighter from Singapore who again was both heavier and shorter than I was. I noticed that I had a much longer reach than my Shaolin opponent, so I decided to try to cut him open above and below both eyes by twisting my punches on impact. He had a tendency to telegraph his techniques. He did manage to trip me once, but otherwise failed to score on me. His cuts were so bad that the fight was stopped at the end of the second round. His face was a mask of blood. He seemed a good man. For a second or two, I was sorry I was so brutal…

Chow Kim-tong had won two fights, but had received similar injuries to me and could only manage 4th place in the middleweight division. Chow never made it to the Olympics. He never fought again after Singapore. He became a Dim Sum (Hong Kong lunch delicacies) chef. He had fought bravely and had got the bruises to prove it.

I'd made it to the final, but my next fight was against Lohandran, the Malaysian Heavyweight Boxing Champ, who had been given a bye in the semi-final when he was drawn against his very own brother. He was going in against me almost totally fresh. Even Sifu said, 'Dan, you do not need to fight again and you have no chance as you are badly injured and he is fresh.' I knew I was going to get a beating, but I told him I had to fight or people would say I was afraid and that would bring dishonour to the school and to Tai Chi. It was the last night of the Championships. It was the last fight of the night.

In the end, I didn't do that badly. The fight went the distance. There were no knockdowns. Lohandran adopted hit and run tactics. All his points were scored by roundhouse kicks to my front leg, which hurt me a bit, but didn't bother me. I hit him a few times. When I got back to Hong Kong, I showed the movie of the fight to Big Don, who was a boxing judge.

He said it looked pretty even. He couldn't call it.

Celebrations

As was the custom, Sifu held a banquet to celebrate our success. The banquet was hosted by Tai Chi elder brothers, Gordon Lee from the Hong Kong and Shanghai Bank and businessman Mr Ng (who died horribly young because of cancer, leaving his wife and young daughter destitute, his Tai Chi family had a whip round for them. We all contributed). Gordon and Mr Ng were also involved in Western Boxing competitions and tried to persuade me to become a Western Boxer.

I politely refused. I didn't want to get side tracked.

Chow Kim-tong and I had to attend the banquet as guests of honour. The two Singapore Merlion trophies were displayed and afterwards kept for perpetuity in Sifu's trophy cabinet I was later given a replica.

The movie of our fights was played endlessly. Our Tai Chi elder brothers, who had never fought full contact, kept coming over to where Chow and I were sitting, congratulating us and then telling us how we should have fought. I found it all deeply humiliating.

It got even worse when I went back to work and had to face my colleagues. The facial bruising took several weeks to heal, while I had a limp for almost three months. It was the first major setback to my master plan of becoming a Tai Chi Sifu.

Bruce and the Spider

It was back to square one, like our Scots warrior king, Robert the Bruce, alone and miserable in a cave, his only friend being an indefatigable spider. I stopped the full contact training, started to work again on my forms and bided my time. I was the spider.

By January 1977, I had been in Aberdeen Sub-Division for about a year when Steve Tang told me out of the blue that I was being transferred to Wanchai Criminal investigation Department (CID).

I was bored with Aberdeen after a year there. I wondered a bit about the sudden transfer and got the whole story later.

I knew Neil R from PTS where he was in one of the squads just ahead of ours. Neil was a nasty piece of work, he had been a City of Glasgow police officer and was around 30 years of age. After PTS, he had been posted to Aberdeen and then to CID Wanchai. Through the grapevine, I had heard stories about his dubious conduct. He was being dismissed for a whole series of incidents involving beating up prisoners and abusing them, he had also behaved improperly to women victims and offenders. I was to take over his team.

Docherty Ya C**T

As luck would have it, I was visiting squadmates Ross and Kiwi at Wanchai Police Officers Mess one lunchtime. I saw that Neil R was at the door. He must have remembered me from PTS.

He said, 'Docherty ya c**t!' and aimed a kick at my groin. I caught his foot and tugged a classical Tai Chi technique 'Single Hand Seize Leg'. He was briefly airborne and being a big, burly man, he came down with a crash, landing on his coccyx. It took six of us to help him into an armchair. All the time, he was shouting and swearing, saying what he would do to me if he had a 'f****ng bottle' in his hand. I informed him that he wasn't capable of doing anything to me, and I walked out.

He knew me as an ex-Glasgow University student, so he thought he could push me around. I'd already been doing martial arts at a high level for six years by then so fighting a bully like Neil was no effort at all. 'You can take the boy out of the Glasgow, but you can't take the Glasgow out of the boy.'

I hadn't expected to end up in CID and was not too happy about it. I was going to be in charge of an Investigation team of one Sergeant, one Junior Investigator (normally a Woman Constable who did the admin) and four Detective Constables who handled whatever cases came up, took statements etc.

Detective Inspector Docherty

Because of ICAC activity against the police force, morale was extremely low, especially in CID. My first DDI (Divisional Detective Inspector), Pete H, was considered a top CID man. His memos and orders were direct and to the point. After Pete H was transferred, he was replaced by Ricky H, another highly professional CID man and Wing Chun Kung Fu practitioner.

Wanchai was the main red light area on Hong Kong Island, teeming with bars, dance halls, brothels, nightclubs and a wide variety of restaurants. There were plenty of crimes reported every day. Each Investigation Team went on reserve duty for 24 hours, from 8 am one day to 8 am the next and had to take the initial action and investigation of each case occurring during their 24 hours reserve. After the 24 hours were up, the OC (Officer Commanding) squad would go to the DDI's office to be ready to answer any queries from the senior officers who received the morning report. We called this 'morning prayers'.

On a bad day, a reserve team could receive up to 30 reports on a 24 hour reserve shift. These could range from shoplifting to murder. Serious cases were normally passed to specialist squads.

The investigation squad on duty had to take any immediate action required before handing on a case. After morning prayers I'd have to take further action on the cases reported or write them off as no crime disclosed. At the end of day two, once all urgent action had been taken, we could go off duty. With a bit of luck, I might get off duty before lunchtime, but normally we ended up going off duty, a good deal later than that. Days three and four were investigation /

Court days normally. We were working around 48 hours every four days. It was tricky work, a lot of old-style corrupt officers were still in the Force and I didn't trust my Detective Sergeant and some of the other squad members.

I was disgusted when my DDI told me that the SSP (Senior Superintendent) Crime Hong Kong Island, Brian W, during his inspection, stated that the way I had handled some cases led him to believe that I was corrupt.

Detective Training School

Fortunately, after five months in CID Wanchai, I got sent to Detective Training School (DTS), on a three-month CID training course. The course covered forensic medicine, criminal law, surveillance, searching premises and people scenes of crime. The course participants were from all over Hong Kong and had like me been serving in the CID. My PTS Irish squad mate, Mike M was also on the course.

We were divided into investigation teams just like the reserve team I'd been in charge of in CID Wanchai. My team's supervisor was Chief Inspector Lai Bun, from Triad Society Bureau. He was a most affable fellow and a real expert on both surveillance (whether on foot or in a vehicle) and Triads. Each team was given four cases to investigate: burglary, robbery, rape and murder. We did a file for each case with witness statements, scenes of crime reports such as fingerprints and would then go on to charge the prisoner and prosecute in court like with real cases.

Another man who made the course worthwhile was a former Homicide Bureau Chief Inspector, promoted to Force Training Officer named, Andy Quinn, from Glasgow. Prior to joining the RHKP, Andy had served in the Palestine Police. He was a huge guy, but a total gent. Highly experienced, and humorous.

His lecture on 'Interrogation' was a classic which began, "If you wish to interrogate a homosexual, you do not begin by asking, 'So are you a stabber or a bender?'" I actually began to enjoy being a detective and found that the option I had taken three years before to study Forensic Pathology was fortuitous indeed.

No Point in North Point

After three months at DTS, I was put in charge of another investigation team, this one was based in North Point, the headquarters of Eastern Division.

Though the area was less busy crime wise than Wanchai. I'd now be doing one 24 hour reserve day every three days.

I didn't get along well with my boss, the DDI Eastern. He was morose, not particularly bright and always thought the worst of everything and everyone, though he wasn't a bad guy as such. I used to wind him up. The DS Eastern was Ron Smith who had interviewed me in Edinburgh two years previously. Unfortunately, he died suddenly and was replaced by a tall, genteel, somewhat wizened Scot called Gordon J.

Odd Couple

Just prior to my transfer to North Point, squad mate, Big Don, was in a serious traffic accident, breaking his leg so badly that aged only 21, he was unable ever to play competitive sport again, so he was transferred to Police Headquarters (PHQ), Planning and Research.

One time, I saw him test a new design of lightweight handcuffs, no way that aluminium crap could restrain Big Don.

He contacted me out of the blue to say that he was intending to apply for a quiet modern, three bedroom married quarter in Chai Wan Police Station on the south side of Hong Kong Island. Because it was a married quarter, he needed a flat mate, so he wondered if I was interested.

I was fed up with living in Aberdeen, Chai Wan would be more convenient for work, so I agreed.

We had some good times together, but he was working 9-5 at Planning and Research in PHQ while I was on reserve duty every three days for 24 hours. I discovered that Big Don had upped his alcohol and cigarette consumption since his accident. He also seemed to live almost exclusively on junk food which he'd bring back with him to our nice apartment, ensuring an almost permanent smell of kebabs mixed with fish and chips and hamburgers. He'd only wash a plate or cup once every single one had been dumped in the sink.

It was like we were the 'Odd Couple' with me being the tidy one.

Fit Up

Around this time, I managed to damage relations between North Point CID and UB (Uniformed Branch). I was on reserve duty one evening when one of the UB Station Sergeants and a few PCs [all dressed in plainclothes] brought a Chinese male up to CID. The Station Sergeant told me that one of the PCs had approached him saying he had urgent information on a suspected restaurant robbery which was scheduled for that night. This PC had been kicked out of CID and wanted to get back in. He said that he knew the robber who would be armed with a knife. The plan was for the PC to arrange to meet the robber in the restaurant at one of the booths.

The Station Sergeant planned an ambush to move in and arrest the armed robber when the PC got up from the table.

It all went to plan. The PC waited in the booth. The robber came in on time and sat down beside the PC, who got up from the table after a bit. The Station Sergeant moved in with his men and put the suspected robber under arrest after finding a bread knife wrapped in newspaper on the seat beside him.

The trouble was that I didn't believe any of it. It smelled to high Heaven like a fit up. I refused to charge the man with anything. I checked and found that he had no previous convictions. Instead, I interrogated the PC who was in no way pleased at the way things had gone.

Relations between CID and UB were at an all-time low. The case was subsequently sent to Hong Kong Island CID HQ for further investigation. The PC ended up in prison instead of the CID.

Bai Guandi

After this case, I was ostracised by many officers in Eastern Division, The worst was when CID Action Squad made some good arrests, and so a 'Bai Guandi' was held.

Bai is the same term as used in Bai Shi and Guandi refers to Guangung (Lord Guan) / Guandi – God Guan (160-220 AD) who is sometimes referred to as the God of War. He was a real person, a loyal general from the time of the Three Kingdoms. He is depicted in paintings and statues as having a red face and black beard, carrying a halberd. His altar can be found in every police station in Hong Kong.

He is also worshiped by triad societies.

At a Bai Guandi ceremony, barbecued pork and other delicacies are offered to the Guandi to thank him for success and good fortunate as was the case in Eastern Division. Supplicants could ask for his help in bad times.

I was blanked by quite a few officers at the Bai Guandi in Eastern.

Popular as ever.

Holidays

I took a week's leave in Bangkok to get away from things. The food and temples were amazing, particularly the statues of the Reclining Buddha and the Emerald Buddha.

Some of the floorshows were pretty amazing too, but I've never really been into that kind of stuff.

A few months later, I made another little trip by boat to Macau and even won some money at roulette though I've never been much of a gambler unlike many of my colleagues.

Racism and Torture

I had another case where a restaurant owner complained to some constables about a customer, a skinny black guy who had eaten in his restaurant, but who refused to pay and was arrested after a dispute. The case was sent to CID.

We searched him and he only had a few coins on him. He seemed to be more or less a penniless beggar. If I charged him, he would probably be given a fine he couldn't pay. It seemed pointless so I released him.

Unfortunately for him, he was re-arrested under similar circumstances a few days later, this time the Detective Inspector handling the case was a racist Antipodean, he and Bob L from Crime Squad tortured and humiliated the guy. Bob subsequently became a sergeant in one of the UK forces and was sent to prison for an attempted fit up.

On the plus side, I had some good officers in my team. I was also able to prove that a fire on a factory premises was not accidental as the Fire Services had reported. I referred to my old copy of Glaister's book on forensic medicine to prove the fire was no accident, so I called in forensics who agreed it was in fact arson. Even the DDI was impressed.

Complaint Substantiated

While based in CID North Point, one of my final cases was the brutal assault of a dance hostess (prostitute) by her partner, a dismissed Detective Sergeant who had become a drug trafficker. She had been beaten up by him in the past and had reported it, but had subsequently refused to testify. I told her we would protect her. When I returned from leave some months later, my boss, Dave Dep SO Ops (Superintendent Operations) PHQ, called for me to go to his office. After I had saluted, he told me to sit and proceeded to read from a file on his desk that had come from the Complaints against Police Office.

It transpired that while I had been on vacation leave, the hostess had not only refused to testify against the man, but had made allegations of her own about me threatening her and forcing her to give evidence against her boyfriend.

Dep told me that CAPO had classified the complaint as substantiated and a formal entry would be made in my Record of Service that I had been reprimanded for my handling of the case. Dep asked me if I had anything to say for myself. I told him that if I had the same case again, I'd take exactly the same action. Furthermore, I pointed out that it was contrary to natural justice for an officer to be reprimanded without interviewing him and allowing him to give his version of events. I said that I found it incredible that CAPO would take the words of a dance hostess and a drug trafficker over a police Inspector.

Dep got angry and said, "You can't say that."

I told him that I just did. I saluted and left.

Police Riot

A few months after I was posted to North Point in 1977, the Royal Hong Kong Police Force finally rioted. Hong Kong has always had a reputation for corruption and many government servants were poorly paid. Police, fire and ambulance staff were infamous for asking for 'tea money' before performing their duties to the public. The Governor, Sir Murray Maclehose, set up the Independent Commission against Corruption which inevitably targeted the RHKP.

Police officers were being arrested on the flimsiest of evidence, often on the word of criminals. Finally, officers all over the Colony refused to take crime reports for three days. More than 4000 police officers marched on ICAC Headquarters, forced their way in, burned files, smashed up the offices and assaulted staff.

The DS Eastern, the kindly Scot Gordon Jack, notified all officers who were Inspectors or above to attend an emergency meeting. He was a broken man. He kept saying, "What's going to happen?"

"We could lose everything."

But in comes the Yin Yang theory of things moving to one extreme before reverting. Sir Murray Maclehose, the Governor of Hong Kong who had unleashed the ICAC, declared a state of emergency and introduced an amnesty. Slowly things started to get back to normal.

After a horrible year in Eastern Division, much of it my own fault, I was very glad to go on vacation leave for four months.

Around The World in Four Months

One of the attractions of working in the RHKP was that as an expatriate officer I received, paid home leave after completing a contract. My first contract was for three years and that earned me four months home leave and, though it was a requirement that I actually return to the UK, I could choose any route I liked. I also earned a 25% gratuity for my three years and four months service.

I went back home via the Philippines, South Korea, Japan, Hawaii, San Francisco, Minneapolis, Ottawa, Montreal, New York, London and finally Glasgow. On the way back to perform my second tour of duty, I visited Amsterdam and then Thailand, which I'd visited while in North Point.

Thriller in Manila

Big Don and I decided to spend our first week of vacation leave together in the Philippines. This was much to the consternation of Don's mum, who disapproved of me and thought I was a bad influence on him.

I probably was.

We checked into a decent hotel in Manila and then hit the town. There were plenty of bars and plenty of girls. I was fortunate enough to meet a nice one on our second day there and spent most of the rest of the week with her. Big Don wasn't too happy at me going with her to Pagsanjan Falls and so on the last night, I suggested that before going out on the town we should check out the hotel bar. Big Don agreed.

As we entered the bar, I noticed the lighting was very subdued. As we sat down, we ordered two San Miguel beers. Gradually our eyes became accustomed to the gloom and as we looked around the premises in the way that only cops know how to do, we noticed that there were no women in the bar, just guys, kissing and canoodling. With other guys. In the bar, I looked at Big Don. Big Don looked at me. We sculled those beers super fast and we were out of there.

We met for breakfast on the last day. I was with my nice student girl, whereas Big Don had spent the night with a pretty rough looking nightclub singer. We'd been hunting for the dark San Miguel beer since we arrived as it is very difficult to get in Hong Kong, We managed to find some and though it was lukewarm, we drank it anyway with the girls for breakfast. Thank God for the beers that torch singer was putting me off my bacon and eggs.

I had a plane to catch.

Room at the Inn

My next port of call was Seoul, South Korea, for a week in the company of Australian squad mate Dave P. There was a substantial American military presence there and you could feel the tension in the air.

Dave met me and told me that we could stay in a traditional Korean Inn for $3 per night. The rooms were divided by sliding panels. Right in the centre of the inn, was a large pond. We discovered that there was a South Korean peach 'champagne' called 'Oscar'. There was also a rice drink called Mokkoli. You could only get it in plastic bottles from restaurants. So every morning, we started with putting Oscar and Mokkoli in the pond to keep them cold.

Dave P had got into town a few days before I did and he told me a romantic story.

Dave was walking along in Seoul when he noticed a girl wearing a micro miniskirt and high heels walking towards him. Just as they passed one another going in opposite directions, Dave turned round.

The girl turned around too, looked at Dave and said, "Short time 10 bucks."

I Am Just a Student Sir

The next evening, we went to a nightclub. As we sat nursing a couple of beers, a pretty young lady wearing a nice frock, came up to our table and said to me, "Excuse me sir, are you an international student?" I saw no reason to contradict her assumption and invited her to sit down. A waiter went past our table and muttered something that I assumed was derogatory to the lady.

White Knight Syndrome

At that time, South Korea was under martial law and there was a curfew. When the bar was closing, the young lady told me that because of the curfew and our location, she'd not be able to get home in time and would be in trouble with the authorities. She graciously accepted my invitation to join me at the inn.

I was shocked at the amount of street violence. My new friend told me that guys would hit a girl if she wouldn't go back with him – a lot of girls preferred foreign men.

Dave and I made a few day trips to ancient temples and visited some great restaurants. We both love kimchi to this day.

Two Weeks in Japan

Time to go to Japan. Japanese culture had intrigued me even when at school and I felt an empathy for it through my martial arts training and the films of Akira Kurosawa.

I visited Tokyo and Kyoto and spent a few days wandering round Mount Fuji which I managed to climb. My legs ached for days afterwards, the last few thousand feet involve clambering over volcanic ash. Fortunately, I had a couple of clear days and enjoyed the spectacular views from the summit.

I visited the famous Budokan (Hall of Martial Ways), where I saw a few martial arts displays, including a ladies only Naginata (Japanese halberd) class.

I enjoyed drinking beer from huge beer steins and eating skewered meats and seafood at the Yakitori stalls. The people were friendly. My landlord in Tokyo had been a prisoner of the Russians during World War II. He did not enjoy his time with them.

God Bless America

I moved onto Hawaii. I had let my hair grow long and shaggy and was wearing a purple and orange Thai shirt and carrying a big red backpack when I arrived.

I should have known better, an oriental looking plainclothes cop stopped me as I was going through customs and searched me and my baggage thoroughly. It took quite some time. Welcome to the USA.

I spent a week sipping cocktails on Hawaiian beaches, I was particularly partial to a Blue Gringo, and somehow it always came out the same colour it went in.

I moved on to San Francisco.

The Family

San Francisco was a charming town with its hills and its streetcars. Great bookstores and excellent restaurants. One day, I was wandering along the old hippy street of Haight Ashbury when I was approached by a friendly couple who invited me to a dinner with a group of friends. I had nothing better to do so, I went along, paid a few dollars for a plate of veggie food and listened to what they had to say. Everything initially was vague stuff about making new friends, living a better life and so on. Like most cults, the discussion leaders were looking for lost souls.

The meeting was drawing to a close around 11 pm when one of the leaders announced that in 15 minutes there would be a bus going to 'The Farm' and newcomers were especially welcome. A nice Japanese girl persuaded me to go along. I never saw her again. A few other newcomers got on the bus and off we went.

We arrived well after midnight at a barred gate, in front of which stood a couple of big guys holding baseball bats, though they didn't look to me like they played baseball. The newcomers, like me, were taken to a large unlit hall, given a sleeping bag, and told they should have a good rest as tomorrow was going to be very exciting.

At around 6 am, we were awoken by a couple of guitar players.

'WAKE UP! YOU SLEEPYHEAD
GET UP! GET OUT OF BED
SEE HOW THE SUN IS SHINING

STAND UP AND MOVE YOUR TOES
TELL THEM IT'S TIME TO GO
YOU'VE GOT A LOT TO DO TODAY.'

So we got up and were asked to go outside and share some morning exercises. After 20 minutes or so, we were given breakfast. By now, we had been separated into groups of between seven to nine people with at most two newcomers per group. The others called themselves members of The Family. We were asked to talk about ourselves. After this we were told, 'Great news! The Principal is going to talk to us.' So we went to another hall. This one looked like a chapel. After some minutes, a be-spectacled middle-aged guy wearing a grey suit and tie came to the rostrum. Immediately everyone stood up – except me. After listening to this smoothy-chopped creep for quite a while, he dismissed us.

I was then approached by one of the leaders who said it looked like The Family was not for me. He said that one of the members was going back to San Francisco that very evening and would I like to go back with him. I went back and that was the end of it.

Uncle John

From San Francisco, I flew to Minneapolis to accept the invite from my Uncle John. I arrived at Minneapolis airport, but there was no one there to greet me. I telephoned his home. One of his sons answered. I told him I was his cousin Dan from Glasgow and Hong Kong and that his dad had invited me to visit. He replied, "My dad died yesterday."

I was shocked and saddened. Uncle John was an exceptional person. My father and grandmother were not well at the time of the funeral so over the phone they asked me to represent them. I felt awkward. My hair was still long and shaggy. I didn't have any formal clothes. My cousins offered a jacket, white shirt and black tie, but I refused the kind offer. My cousins were all good people but I was wasted by my travels. Anyhow, I had nowhere to go.

One of my favourite comic dirges is the Tom Waits classic 'Christmas Card from a Hooker in Minneapolis' The unhappy hooker speaks of all her old friends being dead or imprisoned. The hooker ponders about returning to Minneapolis, this time for keeps.

No chance, Mr Tom Waits.

Mea Culpa Mea Maxima Culpa

After a week of mourning, I flew to Ottawa via Toronto to see my ex-Mountie pal Dave.

Again, my hair was still long and shaggy. Again the backpack, again the colourful shirts. Yet again trouble with customs.

Good thing, I'm not a druggy. The Canadian customs officer is old school, 50ish, an ex-cop. He doesn't believe me when I say that I am an inspector in the RHKP. He doesn't believe the verification of identity memo from PHQ. He searches everything.

Feel like I'm like the Sidney Poitier character, Virgil Tibbs, from the movie, 'In the Heat of the Night'.

Of course, I miss my flight, but finally arrive in Ottawa. This was all my own fault. The days of long shaggy hair and loud shirts were over, but I remained chained to the wheel.

Drink Canada Dry

I see a huge sign in the Arrivals Hall. DRINK CANADA DRY.

I resolve to do just that, soon as I made it to Dave's place.

He had been fortunate, he had married Nancy, a good woman whom he had met in Hong Kong. They lived happily together for many years until her death after a long illness.

The first couple of days, we just played pool and drank beer. I'd never played pool or any other pub games till I went to Hong Kong. Not so Dave, who liked to play for money.

One day, he suggested we go horse riding. Having honed my skills in my youth on the bucking donkeys at West of Scotland seaside resorts such as Largs, I figured I could handle it.

When we arrived at the riding school, we were told that there would be no horses available for a while, unless we were willing to ride bareback. I let my ex-Mountie pal make the call, "Bareback ay? No problem."

I mounted my lovely white horse, the stable hand gave me the reins, slapped the critter (we are in North America remember) on the butt and it took off like a bat out of hell. It looks so easy in the movies. I tried the old martial arts horse-riding stance and not pulling too hard on the reins. I began to realise these nags were more of a challenge than the bucking donkeys of my youth. I went flying off the beast. Dave was so overcome by what he saw happen to me that he started laughing uproariously in his usual empathetic way, he fell off his hoss too and was later to empty the comments of his stomach in the lobby of his apartment block.

White Horse Philosophy

During my eight months at the Royal Hong Kong Police Training School, I got to know Chinese people for the first time and made a lot of new chums.

Two of my new friends, Hon and Ip, were ex-Sergeants who had been promoted to Inspector. They were old guys, more than 30 years of age. They'd often invite me to have a drink with them in the officers' mess after duty. The first time, they said to me, 'You're from Scotland, so you must like whisky. How about White Horse?' So we ended up each time ordering three White Horses. They were always laughing when they made the order.

Later, much later, I learned the fourth century BC Chinese philosophical paradox from the School of Names, 'A White Horse is not a Horse.'

Later, still I learned the Cantonese saying, *Baak Ma Haak Cha, Woo Gau, Dun Deung* (White Horse Black Penis, Dark Prick).

White Horses are a rarity. With other horses, the penis is not so noticeable. With a white horse, the penis is very noticeable, egregious even. Someone who is called 'A White Horse' is considered outrageously naive and ridiculous.

It's been years since I had a White Horse.

It's been a while since I rode bareback. Maybe I'll give Dave a call.

Montreal and New York

I decided it was a good time to get a haircut and buy some new shirts.

I'd had enough of customs officers.

Time to unchain that damned wheel.

From Ottawa, I went to lovely Montreal for a couple of days to see the Heights of Abraham then spent a week or so in New York. I liked it in some ways more than San Francisco: the bookstores, cinemas and restaurants.

London Calling

I had already agreed to do another contract with the police consisting of 30 months followed by three months leave and then another 30 months with another three months leave. Naturally, I hadn't told this to my family.

I spent a few days in London seeing my brother, John, then back for a few weeks in Glasgow. I met all the family again and did some beer drinking with my brothers. They and my sisters had changed too. I felt more of an outsider than ever.

Things were changing in the UK, punk rock was in vogue. I liked some of the music, especially the Sid Vicious version of My Way, but I couldn't relate to the lifestyle.

Big Dan

I guess more than three years of Hong Kong, the RHKP, Tai Chi, and kung fu fighting had changed me more than somewhat. My father now referred to me mockingly, behind my back as Big Dan. I had filled out and was more confident – even brash.

I went to see Al Doran, my old karate master. He was friendly as ever, but we'd both moved on.

I also went to Edinburgh to meet another Scots disciple of Sifu Cheng, Ian Cameron, who had been in the band of the Black Watch Regiment and had spent three years in Hong Kong doing Tai Chi. He was a quiet gent, almost self-effacing.

I realised I was still nowhere near good enough to become a professional Tai Chi Chuan instructor.

I left Glasgow a second time with no regrets. I went to Amsterdam for a week, during which time I saw Pasolini's revolting film, 'Salo, The 120 Days of Sodom.' It was so disgusting that I almost walked out.

From Amsterdam I went to Thailand again, but this time I went to Phuket, as well as Bangkok. The street food was phenomenal and the bars and clubs were fun, but I'd seen enough. I was back on mission.

Second Tour

On my first night back in Hong Kong, after vacation leave, I met up with Aussie Dave and Big Don. We started off by drinking 2 x 1 litre bottles of Johnny Walker Black Label whisky, followed by a bottle of Mekong Thai whiskey. We. Then hit the Wanchai red light area. Next thing, I knew I found myself on what I took to be the lower deck of the Harwich to Holland ferry and spent quite some time looking for my cabin. I followed a group of oriental sailors who were going to the upper deck. From my new vantage point, I could see that I was on an Indonesian freighter in the middle of Hong Kong Harbour. Dawn was breaking over the South China Sea. It was morning.

I followed the sailors onto a small boat which took us to Yaumati Typhoon Shelter. The orientals disembarked. I disembarked. No one said a word. I quit drinking for three weeks after that.

Apparently, I'd left my pals in a bar after telling them that I wanted to get the last ferry back to Kowloon side. But I learned something from the experience. Reckon it was the Mekong. Never went back to Thailand.

CPM

The next day, I found I'd been posted to the Colony Police Military Command and Control Centre, CPM situated at Police Headquarters, Irish Mike M and Baton of Honour winner, Ross were also posted there on the Police desk. On the Military desk, there was an officer of Captain / Major rank or Navy / RAF equivalent.

It was shift work, but only eight hours and there were four of us. Mostly it was a breeze, but we had to liaise with the regional police control centres when there was a major incident such as the sudden influx of Vietnamese refugees. We also dealt with CASEVAC (casualty evacuation) with our military colleagues and had to prepare a report each morning which went to all senior officers from the CP down.

I spent most of my six months at CPM in daydream mode, Weekdays from nine to five, I kept an open file on the desk in front of me so that I looked busy. Our Chief Inspector was Welsh and a super keen twit. He didn't like us inspectors.

We nicknamed him, 'Peter Perfect', after the cartoon character from Wacky Races.

After my last shift at CPM, I invited a nice civilian Chinese messenger girl for a drink in Wanchai. We ended up back at my place. Hmmm, not sure how that happened.

Dan Can't Teach Tai Chi

I sometimes used to practice Tai Chi with Sifu's two sons, Ah Yan and Ah Chiu. One day, I was trying to teach sabre form to Ah Chiu, the younger son, when he reached as far as he had learned. I tried to show him the next technique, but I got it wrong. Sifu loudly said, *Ah Dan m sik gaau Tai Gik* (Dan doesn't know how to teach Tai Chi). He and the students just laughed. I wasn't laughing. I felt humiliated, they were right, I didn't know how to teach Tai Chi.

But I was determined to learn.

Not Again

After Colony Polmil, I was posted to head yet another CID reserve squad, this time in Yaumati on Kowloon side. It was one of the busiest police stations in the Colony.

Two of the senior CID officers with whom I worked there, ended up in prison for sexual offences.

One of them was arrested just after being promoted to Chief Inspector and being made OC Protection of Women and Juveniles.

He had gone to a seedy apartment house in Kowloon, the kind that rents rooms by the hour. He had produced his warrant card at reception and announced, *Cha fong!* (Room inspection).

He inspected three rooms. Each room was occupied by a man and a woman. Each time he told the man to leave and to close the door behind him. He then would indecently assault the female occupant. Someone called the police. An old pal of mine from N squad, Danny C of EU / K (Kowloon Emergency Unit) got his patrol car there pronto and arrested him.

When the case went to court, this gent tried to use his freemasonry on the judge (also a mason) who referred to my ex-boss as, 'A devious manipulator of untruths.' The man was witty, intelligent and charming, but had a limp and a beer gut. He liked to personally interview female defendants, witnesses and victims in his office with the door closed.

Last, I heard he got a job as night security manager at a big hotel.

Nice.

Tea for Two

The other officer, from the North of England was married, but had forced one of the Chinese police station cleaners to have sex with him. She then told her husband who said that he had lost face and demanded compensation. The Gwailo officer refused. The cleaner reported rape and the Gwailo was convicted as charged and spent a few years in prison.

Last I heard, he was selling exotic teas.

New Morning

In April 1979, after two months in Yaumati CID, the District Commander, a pleasant Irishman, told me that I was being transferred to the newly formed Mass Transit Railway Division with effect from Monday. I was happy to hear it. I had enough of CID – and of Yaumati.

The ex-army, old style MTR Divisional Superintendent was Mike Harris whom I knew from Polmil.

Roxy

As we sometimes did after a late supper, Sifu and I went one night with some Chinese martial arts folks to a fancy nightclub in the tourist haven of Tsimshatsui. Some hostesses came over to see if we wanted to offer them over priced hostess drinks. I had no interest and ordered a glass of Martell XO Cognac for myself instead.

Suddenly, I found myself talking to the prettiest and classiest woman in the club. She told me that she was 23 and that she had a regular job as a receptionist, but was trying to be a secretary. She was new to working in a club and not keen on it, but the extra money was useful. I was, somewhat, morose at that time. I wasn't sure if I was ever going to get a chance at full contact fighting again and I'd almost forgotten my dream of becoming a professional Tai Chi teacher. My career in the police was going nowhere while my sex life was non-existent.

White Knight Syndrome 2

I suddenly realised that 'Roxy' (not her name, but it will do), was rather a nice person and in the time we'd been talking, she'd made no effort to get me to buy her a drink. Finally, she asked where I lived and was pleased to hear it was a short cab ride from the club. She was living far away, on Hong Kong side. She asked if she could stay over at my place after the club closed. .

We waited, the club closed and I bade farewell to Sifu and the Kung Fu folk then Roxy and I went off into the night.

MTR

We got up early next day and arranged to meet again, I then headed off to Ngautaukok Police Station, HQ of MTR Division in the East Kowloon belt of high-rise estates, to report for my first day of duty.

I met Chief Inspector Wong and 7 Bongbaan Jai (Little helper and controller) i.e. probationary inspectors with less than three years' service who had only 1 pip / star on each epaulette – I was the only full Bongbaan [2 pip / 2 star Inspector].

We, inspectors and the station sergeants, had to attend several weeks of lectures on the trains, the stations, predicted problems and passenger numbers. The entire project was essential to Hong Kong maintaining or even enhancing its position as the business hub of South East Asia. The whole transit system needed to be overhauled and modernised. The key was the MTR Hong Kong, being a British Colony, most of the senior personnel and machinery they brought in was British, but they wanted all the security, policing and crowd control to be put under the aegis of the RHKP.

The key RHKP man in all this was Mike Harris from the West Country (one of our nicknames for him was 'Rambling Sid' – BBC Radio four-spoof folksinger). An ex-soldier, he was jowly, moustachioed, lecherous, beer bellied, punctilious and indefatigable. His dress sense was so bad I sometimes referred to him as 'The Russian refugee'. I told him so.

He said, "You're a c**t, Dan."

I just said, "Yes sir."

Most of the Bongbaan Jai and the PCs and sergeants had just finished serving in the same Police Tactical Unit

Company (anti-riot). No one was taking any chances with this one. It had to work.

A Multitude of Sins

After the sergeants and PCs had been given a truncated introduction to the MTR, they were separated into four operational units, each commanded by two inspectors. I was partnered up with a dapper-looking Chinese Bongbaan Jai called Sheriff Syn.

No really. His Chinese name was Syn Kam-wah (Syn of Golden Brilliance). Two of his brothers were also members of the RHKP. We referred to them collectively as a multitude of Syns.

Sheriff was a gambler and a womaniser, though not necessarily in that order. He even gambled with the PCs. Things got so bad that even I warned him about it.

He was not exactly a pillar of rectitude, but I loved him like a brother as he was witty and highly intelligent. He dubbed me 'The Saint' as I didn't smoke, didn't gamble and didn't use hookers…

Aut Nunc Aut Numquam

Sheriff and all our sub unit of 30 or so knew that the crazy foreign devil inspector was going to represent Hong Kong at the Fifth South East Asian Chinese Full Contact Championships in Malaysia.in April, 1980. I guess Mike Harris did too, because I was sent on an intensive 11 week Intermediate Level Cantonese language course which ended the day when the competition started. I'd already done a few weeks preparatory training. Now, suddenly for the first time in years I was working nine to five learning more Cantonese. Sheriff was the only friend who really believed that I could do it. He gave me a telling off one night when he caught me drinking beer.

Because of the Cantonese course I was sleeping better, eating better and training better.

I got a credit in my oral Cantonese exam, went out and took a taxi to the airport, got a flight to Penang.

Went for my pre-fight medical that night. The doctor told me, I had a heart murmur, but said I'd be allowed to fight.

Last Chance Saloon

Despite Sifu's protestations, I jumped up two weight divisions to Open Weight (over 220 lb) I only weighed 190lb. I had the fastest and hardest Running Thunder Hands in the Hong Kong Tai Chi school and I'd do more than half a million reps in under 100 days.

It was a no brainer, go up against the big guys, only faster and much harder than them. I hadn't fought full contact for three years and four months, but you never lose it, right?

My Tai Chi elder brother, Tong Chi-kin, was my training partner for 100 days. Kin had a couple of preparatory fights and, unlike me, he'd been training full time. The championships was a chance too for him to honour a dead friend and one time best of Sifu's South East Asian Chinese full contact champions. A man I had never met, who'd won at heavyweight though, he only weighed around 170lbs. With typical insouciance (as we say in Glasgow), I thought, No problem. What he, who had died in a gas leak in 1974, had done, I can do too.

I'd forgotten about the Jade Emperor.

Kin had a harder route in the Middleweight Division than I had in the Open Weight. He had to face four opponents, I had to face two.

Every one of his fights was a war of attrition. Somehow, he eventually beat down and broke down the resistance of all his opponents. The stand out moment was after the first round of his semi-final against the local champion in Ipoh. He was down and badly concussed. I called him over to his corner. 'The other guy is getting tired', I lied. I told him not to sit down so his opponent could see that after being knocked down five times in round number one, he was ready for more.

By this time, things looked so bad, that the local Ipoh Tai Chi fraternity were now supporting the local champ who practiced Chikechuan, a mixture of Thai Boxing and Choy Li Fut (a Chinese martial art which used heavy swing punches).

Amazingly, gradually the tide turned and Kin stopped the local champ in round three. I noticed the local Tai Chi guys had rejoined our camp, now we were successful.

The Harder They Come...

The full contact road show moved on to the one horse town of Seremban. Our Hong Kong delegation arrived late at night and we were shown to our rooms. Sifu and his Tai Chi entourage (Cheng Kam and a business pal of his) refused to take their somewhat dilapidated rooms and ended up in a brothel as nothing else was available. All three of them managed to 'fire their cannons' in each of the four towns hosting the competition. I'd been through these movies with Sifu before. Kin and I were well rested in our very basic room.

The guy I was drawn against was from Five Ancestors Kung Fu (named after five patriotic Shaolin monks who wished to depose the Manchu Qing dynasty and restore the native Chinese Ming dynasty). His name was Roy Pink and he'd been a British full contact champion. Years later, I became friendly with his Sifu, Kim Han. Roy was massive, he weighed more than 300lbs. A friendly Malaysian referee told me that Roy's favourite technique was the spinning back hook kick. I thought no way, a guy Roy's size could do that kick, I knew it well from my karate days.

The fights in Seremban took place in an open-air arena in dark night. We wore red or green T-shirts, long black trousers and a groin guard. We could choose our Thai boxing gloves from a pile, we found out later that the Malaysians had employed top professional Thai Boxing coaches. I chose the lightest pair I could find. I wanted Roy to feel each Running Thunder punch.

Roy and I were top of the bill, last fight of a disastrous night for the Hong Kong team, who had lost every fight except for Kin. I was in red again. I felt invincible.

I jumped up onto the platform. We bowed left palm over right fist to the referee and to one another. The fight started with Roy punching me three times to the head. He didn't hurt me, as I was making a strategic retreat at the time, but he followed up with a spinning back hook kick. I went flying off the Leitai for the first time in my life, but curled up and landed well, going into a backward roll.

I could hear the Jade Emperor laughing, less than five seconds into the fight and despite having been warned about it, Roy's hook kick had humiliatingly got me taking the count.

I could see Big Roy was waiting to give me more of the same. I decided to get up on the count of eight. I knew that now I wasn't strong enough to tackle Roy's huge weight advantage; head on car crash Tai Chi was not an option against a juggernaut like Big Roy.

Champ Dancer

Maybe the Jade Emperor was testing me, but I always practiced footwork from the time of first meeting Nanbu, back in '72. I rarely listened to advice – my speciality was strategy at short notice. I decided to try moving in and out and side to side. Big Roy tried to chase me, but as I had suspected, a guy the size of Roy found it difficult to turn and change direction. We clinched once and I hit him with a Tiger Embrace Head hook punch to the head, just to let him know I was there.

I kept up the Scottish Highland Dance routine.

A few seconds later, Old Twinkle Toes Docherty suddenly went in when Roy was expecting me to go out. Roy walked into a right hand Running Thunder Punch. I saw him go cross-eyed, teeter for a moment then fall flat on his back, unconscious before he hit the ground. The whole platform shook. The punch was so hard that he only woke up in the ambulance. He was a brave man and deserved respect because three nights later he was back fighting for 3rd place.

After the fight I had a couple of Anchor beers to celebrate. Next stop Kuala Lumpur against my old nemesis, Lohandran in front of his own people.

Southpaw Showdown
in Kuala Lumpur

Kin's fight in the Middleweight final was his best in the tournament, he was so determined to take this one last chance to honour his dead friend. Kin is one of the bravest men I ever met. I cannot repay the blood, the sweat or the tears. 100 days of conditioning training together. I was so happy for him.

The stadium was packed full of Chinese people. Lohandran and I were in the last fight of the night, which had again been a disaster for the Hong Kong male fighters, Tong Chi-kin was the only champion.

I had a theory about Lohandran. Most fighters are really only effective on one side and just don't know how to deal with southpaws. My Sifu was left-handed. Ever since, I was a beginner in martial arts I had trained my left hand and side so I could fight southpaw.

I quickly found that Lohandran was nonplussed when he had to fight against a southpaw. His left foot roundhouse kicks were completely ineffective. Maybe that was why he kicked me in the testicles early in round one. I wasn't hurt, but I complained to the ref, who just signalled us to carry on. I waited till the start of round two to reciprocate with a groin kick of my own. Lohandran didn't flinch.

The fight went three rounds, but I got big points by throwing him off the platform a few times. At the end, Lohandran graciously conceded defeat in his home town and presented me with his Malaysian team T-shirt. I still have it. The fight was a bit of a snooze fest. He had tried his old hit and run tactics and they didn't work against the upstart Scots Tai Chi southpaw.

I never fought full contact again.

Aftermath and White Knight Syndrome three

After the fight, I got straight out of that sweltering stadium. I went back to the hotel to shower and change. I'd taken the opportunity before the fight of making private peregrinations in the vicinity of our hotel and I'd met this Cantonese speaking Chinese girl named Florence, who worked in a store and was a Frances Yip (Hong Kong pop starlet) fan like me. She was lamenting the fact that her idol was performing in Kuala Lumpur the very next evening, but she couldn't afford a ticket.

No problem, Florence. We went for dinner at a swish Chinese restaurant and the owner came over. He'd actually been at the fights and he invited us to have a celebratory drink. Florence was delighted.

When I got back to the hotel, Sifu wasn't too happy. He'd wanted to have me on hand for a photo-fest with our Tai Chi uncles. Sorry Sifu, just needed some space.

The uncles were ecstatic, their Tai Chi nephews had undeniably done the business. They would dine out on this one for years. The next night, I used the old tactic of telling everyone how I'd be late for another excruciating dinner as I was 'tired'.

Yep, Florence again.

As we say in Glasgow, *Amor vincit omnia.*

Back in the RHKP

When I got through Immigration at Hong Kong's Kai Tak Airport, the Chinese language TV channels were there to interview me in Cantonese. For the first time I was treated by the local Hong Kong Chinese as someone they were proud of; me, a Scots colonial police inspector South East Asian Chinese full contact champion.

I headed back to my flat, I found on the table a single red rose in a glass of water and a note from Roxy. Very nice, but how did she get into my flat – I'd never given her a key or had I?

Bea and Roxy called me to offer their congratulations. Sorry ladies, I had things to do, places to go, people to see.

Our Team Leaders, a wealthy Eurasian lady and her ex Station Sergeant husband, had offered a bounty of $1000HK to any team members who took 1st place. I couldn't take the money so I used it to invite the team to a banquet. Out of more than 25 Hong Kong fighters, Kin and I were the only ones to take gold.

My photos appeared in the Chinese press reports on the competition. When I returned to MTR, even Mike Harris seemed proud to have me under his command. He phoned up Offbeat, the Force newspaper, and they did a story on me in both Chinese and English. Harris told me that the PTS Commandant wanted to know if I'd like to be the self-defence instructor at PTS. I told him that if he wished to transfer me, I would not object, but I preferred to stay with my unit at MTR.

It was good to be back in the MTR Division, good not to have to do more than two hours a day full contact training, good to get the monkey off my back.

All Things Come...

On my return, Sheriff Syn asked me to be his best man at his wedding, a great honour, especially for a non-Chinese. I accepted his invite, but asked him if he would have still wanted me as best man if I wasn't a South East Asian Full Contact Champion.

Syn just gave his usual enigmatic smile.

The best man's job was to help the groom to get the show on the road and to preserve order. All Syn's old PTU colleagues were invited. One of them, a fat English guy nicknamed Panda playfully tugged at my tie. I just smiled and suddenly pointed away from me and exclaimed, "What's that?"

I then elbowed Panda in the solar plexus.

Nemo me impune lacessit as we say in Glasgow.

Rosetta, the lovely bride (also a police inspector) burst into tears. Syn just smiled.

10000 DAYS.

There is a saying in Chinese martial arts, "Spear 100 days. Sabre 1000 days. Sword 10000 days."

This accurately reflects the degree of difficulty of each weapon.

I had to learn the sword three times from Sifu. The first time was just before vacation leave. The second time I forgot the sword form was because I had to prioritise full contact training. I finally got it with Ian Cameron, who was visiting Hong Kong over three days of sword tuition from Sifu. He again talked of linking techniques. Again, I was dubious. Sometimes a theory is as bad as a lie.

The Lonesome Death of
John Maclennan

The John Maclennan case was one of the most shameful in the annals of the RHKP. John lived a few doors down from me on the fourth floor of Homantin Service flats. Many inspectors who worked in Kowloon lived there.

John came from rural Ayrshire, near my home town of Glasgow. He was a few years older than me and had served a few years more in the Force. Occasionally, we'd chat at the bar in Homantin or exchange pleasantries in our shared corridor. He seemed to be one of life's conservatives. He was medium height with a stocky build. Smart shirt and tie type. A bit dull, Decent enough not that bright, even somewhat boring.

How little we knew him.

John had been told by his boss at Homantin Police Station to report back to him the next day i.e. January 15, 1980, at 9 am as the Special Investigation Unit (SIU) officers were coming to interview him. The SIU was responsible for investigating homosexual activities of government servants and that included police officers. In those days, Sodomy was a criminal offence.

Maclennan went to the armoury in the wee wee hours and signed for a revolver and six rounds of ammunition.

He didn't show up the next morning at 9 am.

They went to see if he was still in his flat.

The door was locked on the inside.

They knocked and rang the bell.

No answer.

They kicked the door open.

They found Detective Inspector John Maclennan with the gun, .38 Colt Police Positive Revolver.

It had been fired five times.

He had five bullet wounds.

John was dead.

There was a suicide note.

They lost it.

They failed to preserve the scene. (of crime or suicide).

It was alleged that he had confidential information concerning the sexual activities of the Commissioner of Police.

It was alleged that he was threatening to go public with it.

The usual anti-police conspiracy theorists demanded an inquiry.

They got one.

I knew John liked women.

He had been interested in one I knew.

It all came out.

John with male prostitutes.

And more, much more.

His broken-hearted mother couldn't take it in.

They didn't have male prostitutes in Ayrshire.

Maybe John shouldn't have joined the RHKP.

Maybe he couldn't take a joke.

Coolie

'Coolie' was the nickname of one of Syn's PCs who had served in PTU with him. As the name suggests, he was a short dark and wiry chap. He had black tabs on his epaulettes, indicating that he was not an English speaker. He had a basic education. He was quiet and hard-working.

Then one day, Coolie walked into the General Office and spoke to me in English. I was taken aback and asked the Station Sergeant about him. He made more arrests than anyone else and was reliable. When I heard there was an interview board for PCs wanting a transfer to CID, I asked Coolie if he was interested. He thought he had no chance because of his poor education. I told him to start wearing his glasses as it made him look more educated.

As his Sub-unit Commander, I had to grade him from A-H on a list of 20 qualities. I gave him A / B for everything except for Turnout and Appearance, for which I gave him a 'G'. I knew the CID Board would like the contrast. He passed and was delighted,

Much to everyone's surprise, after a couple of years in CID, he switched back to Uniformed Branch (UB) by opting, at my suggestion, to attend the PC – Sergeant Promotion Board. He eventually became a Station Sergeant to general amazement.

The story didn't end well as his gambling got out of control and he gave up his position in the Force to become a taxi driver and even gambled away his house. I think I can hear the Jade Emperor laughing. It's presumptuous to think you can help folks.

Demons' Playground

Sifu had a theory about little demons who get their kicks by going around blinding and deafening ordinary folk so as to cause accidents. I didn't subscribe to his theory until one night.

After I finished with Chinese full contact fighting, I asked Sifu Cheng to teach me how to be a Chinese full contact judge. I duly learned. Shortly thereafter, Sifu organised a Chinese Leitai competition in Wanchai. I was one of the judges.

The night began with some demonstrations. A youngish Sifu came onto the Leitai to demonstrate Double Nine Section Steel Whip (basically two steel chains with spearheads at the ends).

He was doing fine, whirling and whipping them out when all of a sudden, one of the whips flew out of his hand and crashed into a small section of wall between two bleachers. Had the whip flown a foot or so in either direction, someone would have been killed.

OK, accidents happen, on with the show.

Next up, a husband and wife demo; Spear (husband) versus Three-Section Flail (wife). Starts off fine, suddenly he misses his Spear defence against her Flail and his forehead is split open and dripping blood. They come off. The tournament doctor bandages the bearded Sifu's bald head. He now looks like a character from the Arabian Nights.

They start up again. She attacks with her Three-Section Flail, he misses his Spear block. Her flail hits his head with a thwack. He is concussed, staggering around dripping blood from his head wound. Suddenly it's bedtime for Bonzo.

No more incidents. Finally, it's the last fight of the night. Two 17-year-old lads, roughly equal in weight and experience. I'm on nodding terms with one of them whom I've often seen train in Kowloon Park. He'd tie a towel round a tree and practice his roundhouse kicks.

It's the beginning of the 1st.

The other kid attacks with a punch.

Roundhouse kick to the neck from Kowloon Park kid.

The crowd goes silent.

Kid unconscious before he hits the canvas.

Dead on arrival Tang Shiu-kin Hospital.

Subsequently Sifu asks me to answer all correspondence from the Legal Aid people who were considering suing our association for negligence on behalf of the dead boy's family.

A few days later, I met Sheriff, who greets me mockingly with my official HK Government name of Tong Chik tak and calls me the 'Great Philanthropist'.

There was no insurance for amateur fighters in those days. The dead kid's family were destitute. We started a fund for them. I donated 1000HK$ which I could easily afford.

Apparently, somebody with good Chinese news media connections alerted the said media to this act of kindness by a Westerner police inspector named 'Tong Chik tak'. It didn't take a genius to work it all out.

Sheriff laughed and laughed.

Martial Virtue

In Chinese martial arts, there is a strong sense of hierarchy within one's own school and fellow students are addressed as younger / older brother / sister. I was not deliberately rude, but often neglected social niceties. My approach to training was serious – not everyone liked that.

I've always tried to keep an open mind, it helps to appreciate good things in other styles. I spent a lot of time with Sifu Cheng going to competitions, demonstrations and dinners so I had the opportunity to watch and listen to top level masters.

Over the years, I have improved my understanding of my Tai Chi by looking at other styles and manuals, occidental and oriental. I always acknowledge useful input. This is an aspect of martial virtue.

Still can't get over Sifu Cheng lecturing me on sincerity one time.

Fat Short and Sturdy

Mike Harris soon realised that he needed an experienced Traffic Inspector to assist and deputize for him at meetings with MTR officials. He got one His name was Dave A.

I'd met him before when he was in charge of traffic on Lantau Island (location of the new Hong Kong Airport). I'd gone there with Mountie Dave, Aussie Dave and some other recruits when we were at PTS.

I remembered this short fat Welsh guy, after a day of beer drinking, driving us all back through the gathering darkness in a police van with siren on full blast and blue lights flashing. He radioed ahead to order the last ferry for Hong Kong Island to wait for us. It did.

I liked this can do mentality.

Maybe life in the RHKP wouldn't be that bad after all.

Dave was an ex-Royal Navy officer, a real character. The late 'Jaws' Luk dubbed him, *Fei Dute Dute* (Fat Short and Sturdy). The nickname stuck.

He was popular and capable, but his tendency to turn up late for duty and to report to lunch at the nearby Kwun Tong Officers Mess at1300 on the dot and stay there for most of the afternoon did not endear him to senior officers nor to his colleagues who had to cover for him…

Orienteering

One day, quite out of the blue, he said to me, "Hey Dan, How about we start an MTR Police Orienteering Club?"

"Say what Dave?"

The idea of this short, fat Welshman running around in shorts, trainers and vest made me laugh out loud, but then he told me that we would get a half day off every Wednesday as the RHKP was keen to have fit officers. I let him handle things and persuaded a few guys in my unit to sign up.

Everything went fine for a while and I enjoyed the tours of rural Hong Kong. I was very impressed that Dave always knew where the nearest police mess could be located.

Came one fateful day, our orienteering club guys were on Hong Kong Island, near Queen Mary's Hospital, it was a scorcher, hot and humid. As usual, I ran ahead while Dave waddled after me as best he could. After a while, Dave called out, "It's too hot, let's walk." So we walked for a spell.

Then Dave said, "Let's sit for a while." So we sat.

Next thing, Dave suggests that we should go back to the start. When we reach the main road, he said, "Let's get a taxi." So we flag down a taxi. Dave sits in the back, I ride upfront. Suddenly, I heard a noise from the back seat, like something falling. I turned around to see Dave lying motionless in the back, staring into space. I immediately redirected the driver to head for Queen Mary's emergency ward. They had to take him in on a stretcher. It turned out he'd had a heart attack.

Some weeks later, my unit were holding a dinner party and Dave was invited as a guest. I arranged to pick him up from the bar / restaurant beside his quarters.

I went to the bar, I waited. No Dave.

I went to his room. From the corridor I could see that the TV was on, lights were on. I knocked the door, no reply.

I was so worried so I asked the Manageress to call him. No answer. I told her about the heart attack, so she brought her pass key, but the door was bolted on the inside. No choice. I kicked it open first time.

A befuddled Dave was lying in bed surrounded by at least three alarm clocks. It was a great night.

Murder in Mongkok

One day, I was with Dave when I was told by MTR Control to attend to an incident at Argyle Station .When we arrived, we went straight to the Police Room (each station had one). There we found two of my PCs with a short, scruffy Eurasian guy who was shouting and swearing in English and Chinese. We managed to calm him down and I was escorting him out of the station when he started up again. I immediately arrested him and took him to Mongkok Police Station to have him charged with a breach of the peace…

A few weeks later, I found his picture in the South China Morning Post. He'd been arrested for murdering his child. It seemed that he had found out his Chinese wife had been having an affair with an expatriate police officer. In revenge he'd thrown his child's little baby body from the balcony of their high rise flat, killing the child. I showed the report to Dave.

We both needed a beer that night.

Death Wish

One night, I was on duty and was chatting with Dave when a 'Bomb Threat' called in. Shortly after this, a suspicious object was found on top of a ticket machine in one of the stations. For safety reasons, the station was closed and the whole line was shut down. It was still rush hour. The MTR personnel were frantic by the time I got to the scene. Though, technically off duty, Dave accompanied me to the scene. He has the experience with explosives from his service in the Royal Navy and was a Police Bomb Disposal Officer, so I was happy to have him there.

We got to the station and were shown where the suspicious device is located. It was a large, nondescript parcel. Dave asks the MTR staff if they could get him a long piece of string. Dave took the string, made a kind of a noose at one end. Being careful not to move the parcel, he slipped the noose over it. We retired as far as we can behind some ticket machines. Dave was still holding the other end of the long piece of string.

Dave tugged his length of string, pulling the parcel off the ticket machine. It hit the ground and bursts open. No bombs. The parcel was full of leftover pork rib bones.

Dave reports to the Control Centre that he has used 'disruption technique' to reveal that the threat was a hoax. The station was reopened and the trains were running again.

We later found out that the hoaxer was a disgruntled MTR employee.

Dave was no intellectual, but was an effective officer and had it not been for his love of beer, he would have been promoted. As he often said, 'Death Wish'.

Saddest Room

After leaving the Force in 1984, I occasionally heard of Dave. Finally, I was told he had got drunk in an expensive hostess club and had bought quite a few drinks for quite a few hostesses for quite a while, using his American Express card, On receipt of his monthly bill, he had refused to pay and had been dismissed for being in a state of pecuniary embarrassment. Later, I found out that there was a bit more to the story.

In 1991, ex Mountie Dave came to visit me in London. I had an address for Welsh Dave in the town of March in Cambridgeshire. Early one Sunday morning, we drove to March. After a few hours driving, we arrived at a pleasant little town with a few nice looking pubs in the High Street. We searched for Dave's road. I'd been told he lived at number one.

There was a number 1 and a number 1A. Which could it be? One house had a neat, pristine garden. The garden in the other was like the Amazonian rain forest. It was a no brainer. No one answered the door when we rang the bell. Being a trained detective and working with an ex-Mountie, I located a phone box and found only one number for someone with the same surname as our ex-comrade. The guy who answered my call informed that at that hour, Dave would be returning from church.

Church?

We returned to the suspected residence and rang the bell. The heavy wooden door creaked opened to reveal a bearded face that greeted us with, "Who are you?" The body was as fat, short and sturdy as ever. After a while, he recognised us and invited us into his front room. It was sad.

As I sat down, I noticed that empty cartons of Benson and Hedges Gold Cut cigarettes were stacked high against each wall, save one area where there was a map of Europe and North Africa pinned to the wall. The map was festooned with black lines and coloured pins. Dave explained that his aunt and uncle were on a cruise and his sole pleasure was tracking their voyage day by day.

I suggested lunch in a local pub, but Dave said he couldn't afford it. We told him that he'd be our guest. He still refused to go to a local pub, but directed us to one quite far from town. We enjoyed his good-humoured storytelling as in the old days. Before we left, I invited him for Xmas. Later, I heard he died alone and penniless.

He was a good officer and colleague, but as he himself used to say after discussing one of his exploits, 'Death Wish.' I never saw him again.

THREE WISE MEN – ONE ARCHBISHOP, ONE MONSIGNOR, ONE CANON.

One day, my father called me to say that our near neighbour back in Glasgow, Archbishop (later to be Cardinal) Joseph Winning, was planning to visit Hong Kong during a Far East tour and could I show him some hospitality. A few days later, the Archbishop called me and we agreed to meet at a convent on Hong Kong Island. I arrived in the early evening at the appointed hour and found a dapper, powder blue safari suited Archbishop holding a man bag. He was flanked by two other clerics (a monsignor and a canon) also wearing mufti.

The first words of Archbishop Winning to me were 'Take us somewhere that serves a good gin and tonic and we'd like to go to an Italian place for dinner. We've had enough Chinese stuff'. I told him that I knew some place and we took a taxi to Lockhart Road, alighting in front of an Italian restaurant just across the road from the Pussycat Club and neon signs that read 'Hostess Bar' and 'Topless'.

My guests seemed completely unfazed by the locality. As we sat down at a table, I ordered four large gin and tonics. The Archbishop chose a bottle of Chianti to go with the meal. The

GTs arrived and were pronounced most satisfactory. The Archbishop said grace. The food and wine came and also met with approval. We finished up and I called for the bill. The clerics ignored it, so I settled up

We left and I poured them into a taxi. It was mildly amusing company for a few hours. The Archbishop made a couple of cracks about my Uncle Ignatius which I ignored. I wasn't interested in his opinions, man bag or no.

Home Leave 2

On the whole, MTR Division had been a terrific posting for me, but it was time for three months of home leave. All my best pals seemed to be married, I was going to be a lonesome traveller.

The Americas

I didn't much like Los Angeles, there seemed to be no heart to it. I spent a couple of pleasant days in San Francisco before taking the horrible Mexican equivalent of Greyhound Bus down to Mexico City and from there went down to Chetumal, near the border with Belize.

I took the Batty Brothers (yes really) bus to Belize City. There were signs everywhere that read 'You better Belize it'. I had a good time in Belize. There was a Caribbean vibe, the Chinese and Indian restaurants prepared seafood dishes which were tasty and fresh and the local rums went down real easy. I spent my evenings at the Crossroads Hotel, listening to Jimmy Cliff songs. After a week, I felt very chilled.

After Belize, I travelled by Greyhound right across the USA to New York. It was stunning. I particularly liked the bleakness of the West and Mid-West.

New York

Mountie Dave had given me the address of a cheap hotel in New York. I gave the details to my cab driver from JFK. He asked, if I was sure I wanted to stay there.

He drove me to a shabby building which had a broken neon HOTEL sign. The vicinity of the hotel seemed to be popular with hookers and belligerent drunks.

Thanks Dave.

I ended up staying at the YMCA

I really enjoyed being back in New York. I found a couple of interesting books including Robert van Gulik's book on Chinese erotic art (I still have it) and went to see some movies.

From New York, I met up with Sifu's nephew in London and went with him to Scotland for sightseeing, before meeting my Tai Chi elder brother Ian in Edinburgh. Kin and Sifu had just arrived from Hong Kong. We gave nine days of workshops which proved to be very popular.

A Good Teacher?

I was clear that Sifu's haphazard way of teaching TCC was confusing. The Japanese martial arts course and grading concept was the way to go. Classes had to be directed and structured. It wasn't acceptable for people to be left to their own devices. I did not confide in anyone on these matters. Time enough, when I had set up my own organisation. Ah Yan, Sifu's elder son by his second wife, once said to me, "My father is not a good teacher, he is someone who knows a lot about Tai Chi."

After the Edinburgh seminar, we spent a few days at my parents' place and then went down to tour London. As usual, spendthrift Sifu Cheng spent the seminar money like there was no tomorrow.

Bob Dylan

After he and Kin left, I hung out with my brother Des and took him to a Bob Dylan concert at Earl's Court. There was no band, just Bob and a piano. It was Dylan's evangelistic period and some irate fans called out the names of some of his early songs. In response Dylan said, "A whole lot of people want to live in the past." To his credit, he sang some old favourites later on.

Paris 2

Afterwards, I spent three weeks alone in Paris working on an English language version of Sifu's 1976 Tai Chi book. I realised that it was not great. It was a prototype. Better stuff was to follow. I stayed near Plee's dojo, but didn't go in. Those days were gone.

Uncles

From Paris, I'd booked to stay in Kuala Lumpur for a week to visit my Tai Chi uncles. They were very welcoming, Especially Uncle Loong Wai-tak, who had been an interpreter for the Japanese during their WWII occupation, He had trained in weightlifting before taking up Tai Chi under Cheng Wing-kwong, Sifu's uncle.

One evening, I was chatting with the uncles about Tai Chi techniques, when one of them proceeded to demonstrate Running Thunder Hand, an overhand strike, which he'd been practicing as an underhand strike for years.

With the brashness of youth I made the mistake of correcting him. It was obvious he'd never used the damned technique.

Sifu had warned me that his uncle changed techniques by telling his students partial truths and convenient lies. In their turn, the uncles didn't believe (or at least said that they did not believe) in the existence of Sifu's other master, the elusive Qi Min-xuan.

Mr. Loong introduced me to a millionaire uncle, who took out and showed me his nickel plated .38 Colt Detective Special which he said he always carried as he'd been kidnapped and held to ransom twice before. He invited me and Sifu Loong to spend a couple of days hunting on his ranch in the jungle. We set out straight away. On arrival we were each given a double-barrelled shotgun.

It was pitch dark as we drove through his fruit orchards (fruits included rambutan, lychee and durian). Mr. Loong and I were sat in the back of our host's Mercedes, shotguns poking through the side windows as we lurched along a dirt road. We could see green and yellow-eyed creatures all around us. I spotted a large bird and fired both barrels. It was a kind of guinea fowl. Fresh curried fowl for dinner with fruit for dessert. The uncles were pleased. The whole of the next day we went tiger hunting with dogs and guns. Thankfully, we only came across wild pigs.

These Young Girls

The next night, after dinner with the uncles, I was nursing a beer in a bar near my hotel when a petite oriental maiden wandered in, and after having a good look around the bar, she came over, sat down beside me and began to talk about the kind of day she'd had. You can imagine my consternation.

I tried talking to her in Chinese, but she said she was half a Malay Muslim, half Indian. She wanted to practice her English.

Next thing I knew, we were back in my hotel room and she was discussing what good Muslim girls do with their body hair. She asked me if I'd like to see.

I don't want to talk about it, except to say that she was a refreshing change from my Tai Chi uncles. I left for Hong Kong the next day, a sadder but wiser man. I realised that I was chained to several karmic wheels which were turning in different directions.

Third Tour

In 1981, after my three months paid home leave, I was posted to Shamshuipo Police Station to a desk job dealing with licences, death reports, etc. My immediate boss was an excellent man called Fung Kwok-ping, whom I respected. He had guts and was intelligent and capable. A few months later, it all changed.

There was a complete reorganisation of the RHKP. A Force Inspection Wing was set up. Their job was to visit Police stations and units with a view to examining procedures, reorganising the structure of the RHKP, creating extra work without any increase in manpower. It's easy being a critic. Everyone's an expert.

Sub-divisions became divisions, run by Superintendents, divisions became districts run by Chief Superintendents, and a lot of people got promoted. I wasn't one of them.

It was often said that the Police Force was Hong Kong's licensed triad society. As with a triad society, internal enemies were often more dangerous than external ones.

Dirty H

I got a new boss, Divisional Superintendent H, who demanded that I take immediate disciplinary proceedings against any constables or sergeants who left cigarette stubs on the station compound. It was clear he was a vicious idiot trying to get me into trouble with the rank and file. His underling, Michael M, (a well-respected exponent of Monkey Boxing) confirmed as much by telling me, 'Every time the boss sees you, he wants to hit you. He can't stand the way you look at him.'

I realised that there was no point in arguing with H, as he was a superintendent and I was only a senior inspector, so I always agreed with whatever he ordered me to do and took no action whatever. It drove him nuts.

The end came when the Commissioner of Police [CP] came to the station on an official inspection. He came to my office with the Kowloon (Nine Dragons) Regional Commander, Jack Johnston, a nice Scots gent, who once told me that I reminded him of a wild Highlander. Dirty H was also there with Mr Lee, our keen and ambitious Chinese District Commander (DC).

After a few pleasantries, the CP asked if we had a Vice Register. We didn't have to have one, but if we did I'd be responsible for it. H and the DC assured the CP that this was a great idea which had their fullest support. The CP then asked, "So Mr Docherty, what is the present situation with the Vice Register?"

I gazed at the CP in a friendly way and said, "The present situation, sir, is that we don't have one, but I'll get it done as soon as I have time."

Jack rolled his eyes staring at the ceiling. The DC and H turned white. The CP just nodded.

Three weeks later, I was transferred to be OC Kowloon Regional Vice Squad. It was a punishment posting in those days with pressure for results from the Operations Wing and would almost certainly lead to allegations of corruption and criminality against me and my officers to the Complaints against Police Office and to ICAC.

9 Dragons International

I guess I was sent there to get into trouble, I did, and I also got to work with some fine officers. I could road test my street Tai Chi skills in the hundreds of drug and illegal gambling arrests we would and did make over seven months. We were given the right to make raids anywhere in Hong Kong, so we were known as Kowloon Gwok Jai (9 Dragons International).

One thing I never did was to use violence against prisoners whether gratuitously or in an attempt to extract information. I made it clear to my squad that I wouldn't tolerate them beating up prisoners either. Whenever a more senior officer asked me to beat up a prisoner, I always told them if they wanted it done they would have to do it by themselves. If I was assaulted or if a prisoner resisted arrest, I'd use 'reasonable force' to control and restrain them.

Why? Partly my karate background. Partly I remembered Gilbert Forbes on the subject of 'Eggshell Skulls'. I didn't want to be responsible for killing or maiming anyone.

Operations Wing

I had a good bunch of senior officers in Operations Wing. There was Aussie Neil, a Narcotics Bureau CIP who had been a few squads behind mine in PTS, we once danced together at an official function (don't ask). He supervised me in major drug cases and gave the squad drug investigations which Narcotics Bureau didn't want to handle.

My direct boss was Pete Grant, ex Royal Navy, a straight and honourable man. I'm sorry I had to lie to these men sometimes, but the alternative often didn't bear thinking about.

Above Pete, there was an Irish Superintendent Ops, Tom Finnerty, another fine officer who at the end of my time in Vice Squad, called me in to tell me he would be going to the Police Tactical Unit as a company commander and wondered if I'd accept his offer for me to be his two i / c (Second in Command). It was a great honour and meant I'd almost certainly be promoted to Chief Inspector. I felt bad when I told him that I had to refuse his kind offer, but for personal reasons, I was going to leave the RHKP after the current tour.

Senior Superintendent, Taff Lloyd, was the somewhat Machiavellian head of Ops Wing. Mostly, I kind of liked him, but I heard on the grapevine he found my monthly reports 'insubordinate' and was considering having me charged under the Official Secrets Act when another police unit found one of my so called 'confidential' files in a premises my team had raided. I was correctly defaulted for this and pleaded guilty as charged.

The presiding officer was Bob (you can call me Sir) Toal, whom I knew slightly and who came from just outside Glasgow. He said that he appreciated that I had been straight with him and I had a reasonable record so he entered a reprimand in my record of service, which was the lightest sentence possible. I told him that he'd been very fair. I then saluted and left the room.

All the Friends
I used to Know...

One of my squad mates from RI 103 had been posted to the Gwok Jai some months previous to my posting. After trying to do the job in the 'old way', he had been dismissed from the police force after an ICAC investigation. He's been a house husband ever since.

The rate of attrition was high amongst friends and colleague, "just because I'm paranoid doesn't mean they are not out to get me."

Ex Mountie Dave, visited me shortly after the posting to Kowloon Vice and said, "Dan, buddy, you got to get out of this place or you'll end up dead or in prison."

For most of the time that I was in the squad, a construction site opposite my block would start their machinery at 8 am. Sometimes, I drank whisky to help me sleep, sometimes I slept on a mat in my Sifu's studio.

In the main, I was my own boss. So long as I got the figures, all was OK. I actually enjoyed the job.

Who You Looking At?

In the squad, there was a very tall bespectacled constable with an unfortunate habit of squinting at people. One night, as we walked past the HQ of the Royal Hong Kong Regiment, he made the mistake of squinting at the sentries. They were affronted by the squint, so, rifles in hand, they chased after him and one of them grabbed his shirt. The squad froze, so I used the Tai Chi Nei Kung technique, 'Swallow Pierces Clouds' followed by a palm strike, to the chest to break the grip, simultaneously admonishing the soldiers to cease and desist as we were the Kowloon Regional mother ******g Vice Squad. They backed off, shouldering their rifles. I was glad I hadn't signed for any of the team to get tooled up with .38s.

The More the Merrier

By now, you will have realised that I abhor violence. One afternoon, I had arranged to meet an Oriental damsel at the Tsimshatsui Ferry Pier. I arrived early, pondering whether the green shirt looked good on me or if red would have been more suitable.

Suddenly, I saw a young Chinese male running towards me. Two other Chinese guys seemed to be chasing him. He tripped and fell a few yards from me. His pursuers caught up and proceeded to kick and stamp their quarry as he lay helpless on the ground. My sense of righteousness was affronted, so I went over and in short order threw one assailant to the ground and put the other in an arm bar. By this time a crowd was gathering, worse still another eight Chinese guys ran up and started to fight among themselves.

I'd never fought more than four people at once, so what to do? Fortunately, a dapper Chinese gent stepped forward out of the crowd as he pulled an automatic pistol from a shoulder holster and told the fighters to stop.

It turned out he was a Sergeant from Special Branch. We got all 11 fighters to line up in single file and marched them up to the nearby local police station where all were charged with 'Fighting in a Public Place'. It turned out they were all painters working on a ship in the harbour. They got to gambling, ending up in a dispute over alleged cheating, leading to a chase and mass brawl.

Never saw that young lady again.

Trust Me, I'm a Policeman

The only vice squad member I didn't like or trust was my Station Sergeant. I knew him from MTR days. He came up to me one time and said that the constable nicknamed 'Tim Tim' (Chinese for Sweety because of his predilection for confectionery), was not suitable for operational work and it was better to keep him in the office.

Tim Tim was a very honest officer, who'd never do anything nefarious. I knew the Station Sergeant was not to be trusted so I said to him, 'You are absolutely right, he is not good on operations. I am therefore going to send him on every single operation that we do, so that he can improve.'

Two Gun Docherty

One hot and humid summer's day, I'd just arrived at the squad's office, when I noticed the Sergeant had a curious bulge under his Hawaiian style shirt. He'd worked with me for nearly two years at MTR Division, so, I knew he was honest and reliable. I asked him to come into the back office and to close the door.

"What have you got under your shirt?" I asked.

"Nothing, sir," he lied.

I told him to lift his shirt. He told me that he could not. I ordered him to lift the shirt immediately or I'd charge him with disobedience of orders.

He lifted his shirt to reveal a .38 snub nosed Colt Detective Special revolver. I was wearing mine. As usual, I had not authorised the squad to draw guns from the armoury except for me, the only person who had a personal issue revolver was the Station Sergeant.

The Sergeant confessed that the Station Sergeant, an avid gambler, had gone to Macau on a gambling trip without permission and had given his personal issue revolver for safe keeping to a not very bright Vice Squad Constable called Kit Jai, telling him that if he carried a revolver in plainclothes, the bar hostesses would think he was in CID and would treat him real good. Kit Jai felt uneasy and told the Sergeant, who tried to protect him by taking the gun from him.

The actions of all three officers were both criminal and contrary to police procedure. It could destroy the lives of the three men involved. Two of whom were very decent fellows.

I told the Sergeant to give me the revolver. After he had done so, I slipped it into my left trouser pocket as a counter balance to my own gun in its hip holster on my right. I told him that if the Station Sergeant didn't return within 24 hours, his gun would go missing and the Station Sergeant would be in big trouble.

The Station Sergeant came back within five hours and rushed over to me to apologise. I told him to shut up and gave him back his gun.

I went straight to Pete Grant's office and told him that the Station Sergeant could no longer be trusted and I wanted him off the squad. Pete started to ask why, but I had a face like thunder, so he told me he'd do his best.

Within 48 hours, the Station Sergeant had been replaced by Station Sergeant Ling, who proved to be smart and courageous. The whole squad was relieved. It later transpired that Ling in his youth had worked with the Deputy Regional Commander, 'Big Bill' Ross, from Glasgow University Medical Faculty. I liked Big Bill even though he was a blue nose (a Protestant supporter of Glasgow Rangers Football Club). Now the squad had another guardian angel watching over us.

Get Real

Don't think I was the gung-ho type. I have always been a cynic. Often times, I'd announce to the squad something along the lines of, "I'm entering in the Occurrence Book that we went off duty today at 1900 hours, it is now 1600hrs. If you are planning to commit any crimes, please do not do so until after 1900hrs." I meant it.

ICAC I Presume

Occasionally, I'd get a job from the friendly Australian Chief Inspector Neil Moody seconded to Kowloon HQ from NB.

One day, he called me up to his office. When I shut the door, he produced a pink 'Confidential' file. He then asked me not to inform anyone in Ops Wing about it.

I told him that I worked directly under Ops Wing. He was ordering me not to tell my bosses what I was doing,

Neil wanted me to do a drugs raid in the Kowloon Walled City. The Walled City was notorious for vice, especially drugs and was a maze of narrow paths and illegal structures populated by criminals, drug addicts and illegal immigrants. People thought it was a no go area for cops. Not for us it wasn't.

I said to Neil that we'd raid the premises very early the next morning. At 4 am, my team met at nearby Wongtaisin Police Station and walked to the Walled City. Its rank odours got stronger as we got nearer.

I was leading the way when I noticed a group of Westerners with radio transmitters gathered by the entrance. I worked out who was in charge and enquired, 'ICAC?'

"Yes," was the reply.

They had already raided our target premises. We went in and found nothing. Only Neil and the squad knew we were raiding somewhere in Wongtaisin. I made a report of the raid and went home for a beer. There was a bad taste in my mouth.

ONE CHRISTMAS CARD, TWO ENGLISH HOOKERS and a PIMP

Sometimes, I was visited at the squad office by an enthusiastic young half German inspector we'll call Heinz.

One day, he rushed into my office to tell me excitedly his vice squad sergeant had info on a drug trafficker in the notorious Chung King Mansions in the sleaziest part of the tourist area of Tsimshatsui. The building was full of illegal casinos, drug divans, hookers and bordellos.

Heinz's problem was that he was only in charge of a district vice squad and he was not permitted to go out of his district. I told him I'd ask Peter Grant if we could do a joint operation. Peter knew of Heinz's reputation and told me, 'You are a SIP (Senior Inspector), he is Bongbaan jai (one pip inspector). He got the info, but you are in charge.'

Heinz was notorious for his Gung ho approach to police work.

Our joint squads set up an ambush – our only clue was that the trafficker was a big and bearded Gwailo and was probably armed. We waited.

Suddenly, I saw some PCs jump on a fat Canadian Kung Fu guy whom I knew from the Chinese full contact competitions. Heinz's squad sergeant had the cannabis the trafficker had sold him. On being searched a knife and more cannabis were found on him, so one of the constables handcuffed the guy's hands behind his back. Suddenly Heinz came running up and proceeded to beat up our peaceful prisoner. I hauled him off and asked him what he thought he was doing.

Heinz said, "I thought he was resisting arrest."

We took the Canadian back to his room in one of the so-called hostels. He recognised me and was very apologetic, saying he'd resorted to selling drugs as he'd run out of money and the knife was only to protect himself against local traffickers as he'd heard they were violent. As we searched his room, I found a Christmas card amongst his letters. He told me that it was from a couple of English 'escorts' whom he knew. There was a reference to drugs on the card.

We went to Tsimshatsui Police Station to charge the guy with drug trafficking and carrying an offensive weapon, after which we went directly to the address on the Christmas card. It was now around 4 am. The flat was nearby. Tim Tim and

Ah Daan, another constable, went up with sledgehammer and bolt-cutters to the door which had an iron grille in front of it. We could see from the corridor that the lights were on inside. I rang the bell and called out, "Police! Open up!"

The door briefly opened and then slammed shut. Suddenly Heinz, who was at the back, jumped into the middle of the corridor and whipped out his personal issue revolver, screaming, "Open up or I shoot!"

His gun was pointing down the corridor with me and my eight squad members in front of him. I pushed his gun hand down and ordered him to put it away.

The door and grille were suddenly opened to reveal a short Filipino guy and two pale English blondes. After we had frisked them, I told the squad to let them sit down under guard as we searched the flat. We found cannabis, we found, heroin, we found amphetamines and all kinds of stuff.

I decided to question them individually in the back bedroom with Heinz. We started with the Filipino. Filipino musicians were no novelty in Hong Kong. Their jobs and lifestyles made drugs a popular sideline.

I started to question him, suddenly Heinz slapped him across the face. I asked, "What the hell was that for?"

Heinz's reply? I thought he was being cheeky. I told Heinz I'd personally hit him if he attempted another assault on the defendants.

He was incredibly insulting to the two 'escort' girls when we interviewed them after reading their correspondence on how they imported drugs into Hong Kong inside their vaginas on unregistered flights. He told both of them that they needed to be fumigated and was less than kind about their porn stash.

After we finished interviewing, charging and bailing our pimp and hooker defendants, I went home. I looked at my watch. I'd been on duty continuously and without sleep for 43 hours. And for what? I badly needed a shower and a Scotch; not necessarily in that order.

Naturally, there were complaints. Guess who got blamed? Peter Grant interviewed me afterwards and asked if there was any truth in the allegations made by the girls' lawyer to CAPO. I just looked him in the eye and said, 'Of course not.'

The Filipino admitted that all the drugs were his and went down for a few years.

The 'girls'? (One of them the daughter of a former Secretary General of Singapore)

They went back to what they did best.

Happy Birthday

My parents came back to Hong Kong in 1982, when I was still in the Vice Squad. On this occasion, I took them on a full day tour of Macao, where we saw all the sites, including the fort, the old cathedral façade, Chinese temples and Jai Alai, as well as enjoying terrific Portuguese food and wine.

They wanted to celebrate my father's birthday, so they asked me to arrange a party at a restaurant inviting some of my friends. So Big Don, Paul To, Irish Mike, Sheriff Syn were among the guests at Hong Kong's only Hungarian Restaurant.

I also introduced them, quite separately, to a Chinese lady, whom I unkindly addressed as 'Suen Mooi', (Sour Plum). Her mum did Tai Chi at the housing estate where they lived. Her Sifu was a Tai Chi younger brother of mine. Ironically, she hated Tai Chi, as she disliked having her beauty sleep disturbed to accompany her mum to the classes. I was later married to this lady and have a wonderful daughter by her.

Paging Mr. Vice

I received a file on a drug trafficker who was an NB target, the info on him was a bit vague. We knew his name and the road and small block of flats where he resided, nothing more than that. Then we tried a vehicle registration check on the cars parked outside the flats. We found a BMW registered to our target with his exact address. We then used one of our vice squad cars to block him in, leaving a message on the dashboard telling him to page us if he wanted to get out. We sauntered off to have a beer. After a short while, we got a call. He was waiting for us by the cars. We identified ourselves as police and searched him, we found packets of heroin in his pockets. We found heroin in the car. We found heroin in the flat. He was devastated that he had actually called the police to come and arrest him. He was sent to prison for a long time.

Domino Theory

Every police force is governed by figures and reports. I had to submit a report every month to my Ops Wing bosses and NB.

Another day in vice, another file to investigate. Information from a Detective Sergeant from Mongkok concerning three opium divans operating in Taikoktsui, near the harbour.

The D / Sgt. wanted to be in on the raids. Whether, this was due to an excess of enthusiasm or because he wanted to put the squeeze on the divan operators, I didn't know, but I was sure I didn't want to bring him along.

We hit the first divan that very night, we could smell the unique sickly scent of opium from the other end of the corridor. We burst in to find around 15 men aged from 40-70 plus reclining on the matted floor. Some were puffing on opium pipes, some appeared to be asleep. Scattered around the floor, were opium, paraphernalia, I had two Bongbaan jai from PTS on one-week attachment to the squad. They were delighted because genuine opium divans were by then quite rare. The Ops Wing bosses were ecstatic.

The PTS lads and the Ops Wing were even more delighted when the squad raided the second divan the very next night, making even more arrests (including a Kung Fu Sifu whom I knew) and seizing more opium than the night before.

The next day, a smiling Taff Lloyd told everyone in Ops Wing that the District Commander Mongkok had called him up to ask what the hell was going on in Taikoktsui and was it the Domino Theory.

I had a chat with Ling, the new Station Sergeant. He advised me not to make it three nights in a row as divans are rare and the following monthly report wouldn't look that good, if there were no divans compared with three for the previous month. Wise words. I followed his advice and raided divan number three on the 1st of the following month. The squad wasn't too popular in Mongkok after all that.

Opium wasn't really a problem compared to heroin which caused a lot of street crime. Hong Kong street heroin was also much stronger than what was being sold on the streets of New York. There were regular deaths due to Hong Kong heroin overdose amongst US Navy personnel when the fleet was in.

Nothing Torn Nothing Broken

I don't usually drink alcohol until the sun goes down. It was my last day on Vice. I'd handed over the squad to a polite English gent from Marine Police called Les Bird. He understudied me for a week then took over. I was pleased my squad had got a real good man as their new OC.

After saying goodbye to Ops Wing, I left to return my personal issue revolver, which I was still wearing. Firstly though, I'd arranged to meet old squad mates Mike M and Big Don for lunch at the Boundary Street RHKP Sports Club. Mike made a joke about getting out of the punishment posting of Kowloon Regional Vice Squad with 'Nothing torn, nothing broken' as the Chinese say.

The Jade Emperor hadn't quite finished with me. After lunch, someone suggested having a gin and tonic to wash it down. Nobody demurred. After quaffing more than one of said beverage, it was time to go.

From Boundary Street, I proceeded in a southerly direction down Nathan Road, the main shopping street in Kowloon. It wasn't any different from any other weekday afternoon. I was wearing shirt, tie, a brown sports jacket and my Vice Squad white Florsheim brothel creepers. Everything seemed tickety boo.

Street fighter

Suddenly, a fist flashed past my head from behind. I guess some kind of sixth sense made me move my head. I turned to face my assailant, going into my customary open handed on guard. I was faced with an average sized Chinese male in his 20's who was wearing dusty blue denims. He was most probably an illegal immigrant from China working on a construction site.

Those guys were strong and rough. Flight, drawing the gun and apology were not options. I kicked him full power in the groin as he came in for a second attempt. He gasped, gathered himself for another go. I kicked him again with the same result, a crowd of Chinese people had gathered by this time.

I knew I had to try something different. I seized him as he came in for his fourth attack and took his legs away from under him using Tai Chi technique, 'Sweep Lotus Leg'. As he went down, he grabbed my jacket and ripped it from coat tail to collar.

I'd had enough of trying not to hurt him too badly.

I hit him on the temple left and right four times. I left the scene immediately, pulling out my shirt tails to cover my gun and getting rid of my ruined jacket. I was not proud of myself.

He was lying unconscious on the sidewalk when I left (possibly dead as each of my strikes was against a vital point).

But I learned something from the experience: Never drink gin and tonic unless you are wearing a quality jacket.

White Crane versus Tai Chi

Cheng Tin-hung's Hong Kong Tai Chi Institute had been famous since 1957 when Sifu defeated the Taiwan Middleweight Chinese Full Contact Champion in Taiwan. His students won local and international Chinese full contact championships. He had always had a group of fighters training, but by the time I arrived on the scene in 1975, the only fighters left were Chow Kim-tong who fought with me in the South East Asian Championships in Singapore in 1976 and Tong Chi-kin who started full contact fighting a bit after me. Kin had two fights after our success in Malaysia in 1980.

A team of Canadian White Crane boxers came over to Hong Kong to take on the local champions. Three decades previously there had been an inconclusive fight in Macau between Tai Chi master Wu Jianquan's son, Wu Gongyi, then in his 50s and his White Crane challenger, Chan Ha-fu who was more than 20 years younger. Wu Jianquan was a famous Tai Chi Sifu who taught my teacher's uncle, Cheng Wing-kwong.

The Canadian White Cranes were intent on proving their superiority. Sifu Cheng didn't get involved.

The final contest of the evening matched the top Canadian White Crane fighter against my Tai Chi elder brother, Tong Chi-kin.

Kin was a bit rusty as he hadn't fought for a while and relationships between us were somewhat cool, so he had inexperienced Tai Chi brothers as corner men. Kin was knocked down seven times in the first round; he was flat on the canvas when the bell sounded for the end of the round.

I could see Hong Kong's top White Crane masters were enjoying the spectacle. With my trademark lack of ceremony,

I went unbidden to Kin's corner and told my Tai Chi brothers to beat it, which they did. I wasn't allowed on the fighting platform, so I called Kin to come to me. Gradually, he regained his feet, still heavily concussed. I told him to stay standing so the Canadian would see Kin had still got some fight in him. I had to give him a plan for round two. The Canadians were essentially kickboxers not used to being pushed. I gave Kin the mantra, 'Punch and push.'

My idea was for Kin to use direct Running Thunder Hand punches followed up by pushing the Canadian whose natural response would cause him to come forward again, whereby he'd be walking into Kin's punches and pushes, starting the same cycle again. It worked. Kin knocked the White Crane Canadian down at the end of round two.

The Canadians and the Hong Kong White Crane masters were furious and complained about our change of corner man, but the rules had nothing to forbid it.

Round three was a breeze. The Canadians were without a Plan B. Kin stopped the Canadian towards the end of the round. The local spectators were delighted at a Hong Kong boy winning such an exciting fight. Some came over to shake his hand and to say, *Ho da Tong Sifu* (well fought Sifu Tong.)

On our minibus back to Mongkok, Sifu told everyone to clap their hands for me, because I had won the fight for Tai Chi. They all clapped furiously. Even Kin.

Sifu where were you?

Requiem for a Middleweight

I thought Kin was through with his Pyrrhic victories. He was so humble, so loyal. Sifu announced one day that a team of North American professional kickboxers was coming to Hong Kong in three weeks' time to challenge the locals. I asked what rules would be used. Sifu's attitude was:

1.   These people are professional kickboxers.
2.   We have to face them.
3.   The rules don't matter.
4.   The Hong Kong fighters will all lose.

Although, I still respected Sifu Cheng, I felt he had lost the plot. He had already contacted Kin and ordered him to fight, though he had a full time job, hadn't fought for months and had less than three weeks to prepare instead of three months. It was madness.

All the HK fighters were amateurs, the proposed rules were a mixture of kickboxing and Chinese Lei Tai, e.g. the kickboxers insisted all fighters bound their hands like boxers, but the gloves used were only 4oz.

I wanted nothing to do with it, but agreed to be Kin's corner man for the last time.

The bell sounded. The referee signalled for the fighters to fight. Kin went forward with his usual open guard and his American opponent knocked him down with his first punch from his Western Boxing bandage wrapped hands.

After seeing the 17-year-old kid die a few months before, I decided enough was enough and for the only time as a corner man, I threw in the towel. For Chinese, 'face' is everything.

Being a Celt I also believe in face, but not at the expense of common sense.

Kin never fought again. All the other HK fighters were destroyed by the professional kickboxers except for Sin Lam-yuk, a talented Monkey Boxer and former SE Asian Chinese full contact champion, he got a draw. It was some weeks before I showed up at Sifu's place again. Nobody talked to me. Kin went back to work, though he soon gave it up to become a Tai Chi teacher. Sifu went back to China.

RCCC / K

As I had less than a year to go of my last 30-month tour, the Force didn't want me involved in any more court cases after Vice Squad, so I was posted to Kowloon Regional Command and Control Centre. It was a huge room compared to Colony Polmil. It was shift work, but only a 40-hour week. A superintendent with two SIP controllers under him was in charge of each shift. There were also civilian staff under him. Each district in Kowloon Region nominated the police personnel for their district desk, There was by then an effective beat radio system, so we could be very busy if we had a major incident.

My team was headed by a tough old Shandong Superintendent, Lo Hung-sun, who sometimes discussed Chinese poetry with me. The other SIP on the team was old squad mate Rita Chu.

Stag Night

One day, I get a call from old squad mate, Aussie Dave. He's getting wed and wants me to go to his stag night at the Officers Mess, 20th Floor, PHQ.

So a few days later, I'm having a beer with Dave at his stag night, when a 'tall, big, mighty and ferocious' woman walks in and is introduced to us as Bonita, the bride to be. We are all sure she will leave us at PHQ, when we head off to the nearby Wanchai, to continue celebrating Dave's good fortune.

She follows us down in the lift. She starts walking with us towards Wanchai. Suddenly Irish Mike says to her, 'You should trust him, you know.'

Bonita replies, "I trust him, but I don't trust you!"

Unbelievable.

She's with us all night.

Bonita calls time well before 11 pm.

Bedtime for Bonzo.

To be fair, they've been great together.

You Said You Were an Actress

I get a call from Sifu Cheng one day. He tells me to come over to the studio as he has a job for me.

When I get there, he introduces me to a middle-aged Chinese gent who was one of his old students and to a young lady, the daughter of said gent.

She told me that she was an actress and that she had just been given a role in a Kung Fu movie which involved a lot of swordplay, although, she had no martial arts experience whatsoever. They would be starting shooting in a couple of weeks and she needed to be able to handle a sword competently by then.

Sifu couldn't do the job himself as he was going to China and he couldn't get anyone else competent to give her private sword tuition at short notice, except for me. Sifu told them that as a police officer, I couldn't take any money for the tuition, but on completion of our daily two-hour sessions, the young thespian would take me out to dinner.

Hmmm teach a beautiful Chinese actress swordplay every day for two weeks, surely I had better things to do?

Oh, alright then. She was my first student and an excellent student she was. The dinner was great. I started to thinking that this Tai Chi business beats being a cop. No contest.

Happy New Year 1984

I only got in trouble once during my posting at RCCC / K.

I had gone off duty on the stroke of New Year 1984 and just missed being at the Homantin residents lounge to see in the New Year. I was stone cold sober and approaching the bar entrance when PB, a fellow Scot and CID man, whom I knew as a boozer and a gambler, accosted me. He'd obviously been drinking. He said, "Think you're tough Docherty?"

We had never had any conflict before so I tried to ignore him, but he rushed me as I was approaching the WC. I used a diagonal seven Star Step Tai Chi sidestep and he went crashing through the toilet door.

When he came out, he was even more aggressive and tried to snatch my trendy Rayban shades right off my face.

I'd had enough. It was only some minutes into 1984 and I was in a fight already. I grabbed PB's right arm with my left hand and pushed him up against the wall, trapping his left arm. I hit him three times between the eyes. Three times because he was a big guy, he told me later that he was unconscious after my first punch. He woke up in an ambulance. He had to wear shades himself the next week as he was prosecuting a case in the Supreme Court.

After the fight, I was sitting in the hallway having a chat with Janet Gafoor, the tough but nice manageress of the Homantin Service flats who had witnessed the attack.

Suddenly, scrawny little VC, one of PB's clique of adoring acolytes who hadn't seen the fight, ran out of the bar. He screamed at me, "You hit PB!" As he tried to punch me with his tiny hands, I took the punch on the cheek and told him he had no power and couldn't hurt me. He became even more angry. And flounced off.

Guess who got the blame? Even all these years later false versions of this 'encounter' and my brutality are being bandied around by ex-colleagues who weren't there, but claimed I'd hit a blameless PB six times.

Last Days

From RCCC / K, I was sent to North Kowloon Magistracy to be a Police prosecutor, my final job in the Force. My initial boss was an experienced Pakistani Chief Inspector, Rab N. I didn't dislike him, but he got on my nerves and I remember putting a chokehold on him, in the Mongkok Officers Mess one evening. He was a bit sheepish the next day, I just acted like nothing had happened. I was a bit bored working in the Magistracy, but I made some good friends there, in particular, Peter Mok, a highly literate and bolshie tennis playing Chinese Inspector, who later got into equestrian activities and cricket.

Albert Camus once said, "No one is guilty because we did not begin history, no one is innocent because we continue it."

He was not wrong.

For some police officers, arresting people and charging them to court is a numbers game. For the person so charged, there was the possibility of having their life destroyed. I prosecuted cases in the court of Mr Corcos, an ex-Old Bailey magistrate. He was generally fair.

Jesus Was a Carpenter

One day, I had to prosecute a young male defendant who had been arrested by two young PTU PCs for 'Loitering' outside some shops and 'Going Equipped for Stealing' – he had a screwdriver in his pocket. The defendant was accompanied by two Chinese ladies.

Things didn't add up. It was not appropriate for me as prosecutor to approach a defendant, so I asked Alice, the Court Interpreter to have a word. Turned out that the ladies were his mother and grandmother and he was their only means of support.

I looked at the case file again.

He had no criminal record.

His occupation was given as 'Carpenter'.

He lived next door to where he was arrested.

Corcos entered the Court.

"All rise."

The case began with me asking one of the PTU PCs, "What is the defendant's occupation?" The PC tried to object to my question, but the wily old Jewish beak understood the implications immediately, took one look at the court file and said to me, "Mr Docherty, you may wish to take instructions."

I called the Reserve DI responsible for the case and told him the facts. The prosecution offered no evidence. The defendant left with the old ladies and not a stain on his character. I got on very well with Corcos after that.

Detail

Usually, I just presented the facts, but some cases got to me. One was an indecent assault on a schoolgirl of 14. The accused was arrested by police just outside the apartment block where the assault occurred. As police prosecutor, I had his criminal record on file. Four previous convictions – all for indecent assault. I was sure about this one. His main witness was his girlfriend, who attempted to corroborate his evidence. My detailed questioning unravelled their tissue of lies. He went down. The girl's dad thanked the sergeant who made the arrest. The sergeant replied, 'Don't thank me. It was Ah Sir who asked the good questions.'

Sometimes, it was a great job.

In the Magistracy, I often saw the guilty go free and saw occasionally the conviction of the innocent.

Cantonese Opera

I met an outstanding person who secretly helped me especially her translations of Tai Chi material from Chinese to English. She was a credit to her gender.

She had the same Christian name as one of Prosper Merimee's literary creations. No, it wasn't Columba.

North Kowloon Magistracy was my last posting in the RHKP.

I did my last prosecution. I said goodbye to Roy N the new OC of North Kowloon Magistracy Prosecutions and handed in my police warrant card.

There was no farewell party. I saw a few friends quietly before leaving.

I went with squadmates Irish Mike and Paul on a two day walk on Lantau Island. We shared the bedding.

I flew back to Glasgow. My father picked me up. He and my mother recommended that I should go back to Hong Kong and rejoin the RHKP. Becoming a Tai Chi teacher was madness.

As usual, I didn't listen.

Back To the Future

After a couple of months in Glasgow –mainly spent at the Mitchell Library researching symbolism, my latest obsession, I flew back to Hong Kong, only to discover that Sifu had sold my $36000 Hong Kong worth of gold which I had deposited in his safe and spent it all on Tai Chi Heights, his very own Tai Chi vanity project theme park back in his village. Fortunately not all my money was in gold.

I can still recall him lecturing me about the importance of sincerity. Hold on. Sounds like the Jade Emperor is having a fit of the giggles.

The East Is Black

China was opening up to Western visitors in the 1980s, it seemed fitting, before my final return to the UK to end my apprenticeship with a visit to Beijing, the Shaolin Temple and Wudang Mountain. Sifu Cheng agreed to be my guide if I gave him 2000 pounds to pay the cost of the two-and-a-half-week trip. I agreed.

Technically being on home leave, I was still in the RHKP and not supposed to go to China without permission but it could be a long time till I came back to the Far East.

We firstly went to Sifu's home village of San Xiang which was in a restricted area in Guangdong Province, and thus not open to non-Chinese. To get there, I had to put in my visa application that I was ethnic Chinese through my grandparents.

I finally got to see 'our restaurant'. The food was good, but government officials and their friends and family expected to eat for free. Sifu later sold the land, without telling me.

Sincerity huh?

One of the first things I learned to say in Cantonese was, *Mo Jak-dung mo lun yung* (Literally, Mao Tsetung has no penis to use). I never used this expression in China though. I had many Hong Kong friends and colleagues whose families were victims of 'The Great Leap Forward' and 'The Cultural Revolution'.

I had no illusions. Sifu Cheng came to Hong Kong as a teenage illegal immigrant. The anthem of the Chinese Communist Party was 'The East is Red' a paean of Mao worship. Given his direct involvement in the deaths of millions of Chinese, 'The East is Black' is more appropriate.

Sifu said Mao was very f*****g clever and very f*****g poisonous. He added that the West is black too. Sifu had his dark side also, even I have a dark side.

Beijing

After a few days in Sifu's village and a visit to the Zhongshan house of Nationalist leader and boss of the Three Harmonies Triad Society, Doctor Sun Yat-sen, we flew to Beijing. The airport taxi driver became our guide to the capital. We visited the Forbidden City and walked the courtyards, palaces, temples and other places where once had walked Manchu nobles and martial arts masters such as Yang Lu-chan who brought Tai Chi to Beijing in 1852 and taught his art to the Imperial Guard as well as to Manchu princes.

We visited the Great Hall of the People, Tiananmen (Heavenly Peace) Square, Tibetan Buddhist Temples, the White Cloud Taoist Temple where Zhang San-feng, Tai Chi's putative founder, had lived, where Tai Chi and other martial arts are still practiced. We went to the Ming Tombs, to the Great Wall, to the Summer Palace where we saw the marble boat built by the Empress Dowager Ci Xi using funds embezzled from the Chinese navy. Maybe it was just as well, the Chinese navy was no match for Western warships.

The original marble boat had been destroyed by British and French forces under the command of Lord Elgin in 1860 during the sacking of the Summer Palace as a reprisal for the torture and murder by the Chinese of members of a British French delegation during the Second Opium War.

Lord Elgin's dad had removed the so-called 'Elgin Marbles' from Greece. Their ancestor, Robert the Bruce, would have been proud of them.

I noted that there is no information on what the Yang or other Tai Chi families were doing at the time of Elgin's attack. They were supposed to be teaching Tai Chi in the Forbidden City.

The restaurants in Beijing, were good except for one place where our attempts to order each dish were met by the sullen response, *Mei you le* (we don't have it). When we asked the surly waiter what they did have, he just replied that we had to order from the menu.

Unlike Sifu's village where fresh fruit was plentiful, the fruit in Beijing was half-rotten while our breakfast orange juice didn't taste of oranges.

Ruins of the Shaolin Temple 1984.

Shaolin

We took the train from Beijing to Zhengzhou and next day took a taxi to the Northern Shaolin Temple at Songshan. Legend has it that the patriarch, Da Mo / Bodhidharma meditated for nine years facing a cave wall at the foot of Mount Song, leaving the imprint of his shadow. I felt some empathy with him as I had given up nine years of my own life in a search for enlightenment. He is credited with introducing Buddhism from India to China in the fifth century AD. He is also credited with teaching health exercises to the monks.

As we walked in the courtyard, a young Chinese guy made a grab for my Rayban sunglasses. I deflected his arm with a Five Element Arm palm strike, just hard enough to deter him from trying it again.

The Temple was a ruin, there were no monks to be seen. There was a training area with indentations on the floor from Shaolin Kung Fu stamps. There were ancient frescoes on the walls depicting Shaolin Boxing techniques. There is also a large and ancient cemetery.

On a later visit, in 1999, I talked to villagers who told me there had been riots around the Temple. A new abbot had taken over and announced that historically all the land in the vicinity of Shaolin belonged to the Temple. Villagers whose families had lived there for generations were dragged from their homes by cops and soldiers. Houses and businesses were bulldozed. No compensation. The hatred of the villagers for the thieving monks was visceral.

One day was enough to see the Temple. There are other Shaolin temples in South China notably in Quanzhou, but the Northern Temple is the main one.

Wuhan

Next, we went by train to Wuhan for a private audience with the Governor of Hubei Province (arranged by Sifu's contacts) to get permission to visit Wudang Mountain. He invited us to dinner. He said that since the revolution only a handful of foreigners had visited Wudang, but there were big plans for improving transport and accommodation for tourists.

He asked me to write about my visit and to come again. I've been faithful to my promise and have returned with friends and students more than 10 times. After a couple of days touring Wuhan including the White Horse Temple – yes there is one, we took a train to Wudang where we were met by a couple of his officials who acted as our guides.

Taoist Temples on the Southern Cliff of Wudang Mountain 1984.

Wudang

Wudangshan is not a mountain, rather it is a range of 72 peaks and covers a vast area. It is the abode of the god Zhen Wu (The True Warrior – Wudang means 'Matching the Warrior'). For centuries Wudang has been famous as a place of pilgrimage, and a source of rare medicinal plants.

Wudang was the first of many sacred mountains that I have climbed. Chinese say, "The mountains are high and the Emperor is far away."

It is the equivalent of, "When the cat is away, the mice will play." On a later visit, a taxi driver if I knew what 'xiaoje' meant. The literal sense is 'Little Sister', it is also a euphemism for prostitute. The driver pointed out a bordello at the foot of the mountain.

There are gangsters on the mountain trying to put the small operators out of business. The usual threats against family and staff.

Wudang has long been a refuge for itinerant Taoist hermits, bandits and martial artists. Successive Ming dynasty emperors built temples, shrines and monuments all over Wudang as they attempted to find the elusive Taoist, Zhang San-feng. As with Bodhidharma, there is also a small cave on the mountain where Zhang is said to have meditated.

As we climbed towards the Golden Peak, with our porters and guides, we met a spry 81 year old Taoist priest, who, in return for three cigarettes, offered to perform some Taihe Chuan (Supreme Harmony Boxing – Taihe Shan is an old Taoist name for Wudangshan). Sifu gave the priest the cigarettes and the old priest showed his form which wasn't that martial or that beautiful to watch, but for an octogenarian, he jumped, kicked and stretched most impressively. In 1984 there were no martial arts schools on Wudang; now they are to be found all around the mountain as well as in and around Wudang Town.

With all that time spent meditating it's a wonder how anything got done. In his novel, 'The Chinese Emperor', Jean Levi has the ancient physician, Hua Tuo saying, 'An hour of study under a master is more rewarding than a lifetime of solitary meditation.'

It took us five hours to climb to the summit, visiting Taoist sites on the way up.

On the summit, there was a lovely bronze pavilion enclosing a life size bronze statue of Zhen Wu seated with a bronze statuette of the symbolically entwined sacred tortoise and snake at his feet

We spent five days on Wudang, visiting the main sites. I particularly liked 'Tian Men' (Sky Doors / Gateways to Heaven). These are huge stone archways which initially seem to be gateways to the summit, but only lead to more undulations. A bit like life really.

All around Wudang, there are stone statues of giant tortoises carrying huge stone stelae on their backs, cautioning Taoist priests and nuns as well as visitors to behave respectfully on the sacred mountain. There was even a Taoist prison for those who didn't heed the advice.

I was very happy with the trip.

We got back to Hong Kong by train via Wuhan and Zhongshan.

It was great to be back in a place with toilets that worked, women who knew how to dress and with real beer.

I then had a quiet wedding.

Shortly after the China trip, I said my goodbyes to Sifu and to friends. I was not to return to the Far East for four years.

London Calling

I spent the rest of the summer with my wife at my parents'
place in Glasgow. To their credit they were both extremely
kind to her. She liked them too.

Soon, we were heading down to London where my
brothers Mike and John all helped us in different ways, apart
from them, I had no contacts in London. I owe much to each.

Miss Chen

At the beginning of my UK home leave, I noticed an ad in The Guardian newspaper for a one year intensive Postgraduate Diploma in Chinese at Ealing College West London. The course was designed to enable participants to do independent research in any subject. It seemed ideal for me. I applied and was accepted. It cost £700. Well worth it.

It had been most useful being able to speak Cantonese in Hong Kong. This new course enabled me to do translations of Chinese texts such as the Tai Chi Chuan Classics as well as being able to speak Mandarin, the most widely spoken Chinese dialect. It meant a delay of nine months before I'd be able to teach Tai Chi full-time.

The course was run by Miss Chen Jingzu who was originally from Sichuan. Her main assistant was a Mr. Tang who was originally from Beijing. They did not get on. Miss Chen was about 60 and so the course I was on would be her last.

She was an excellent teacher. I was one of the few she never shouted at.

Hot Potatoes and Idiots

Every Monday morning, Miss Chen had a three-hour class to analyse our translations of a prepared text. Mr Tang called this 'Eating the hot potato. ' Miss Chen would get very angry if she felt a student hadn't been working hard enough and she'd shout, "Nonsense! Rubbish! You are an idiot!"

A few of the young lads on the course who were recent graduates complained to me about Miss Chen's insults. I said to them, 'Do you want to get your Chinese Diplomas?'

They all answered in the affirmative.

I then asked them, "Did you prepare the text for Miss Chen's class?"

"Errh, no."

"Then you are a bunch of idiots."

Stupid Boy

Some of my classmates were not that bright. Patrick was a nerdy little guy who always wore his spectacles. We were reading out our translations of an account of The Long March. When little Patrick's turn came. He blurted out to Mr Tang that he couldn't manage to translate the passage in any way that made sense.

It took a while to work out that though Patrick had correctly read the Chinese text in vertical sequence from top to bottom, he'd been reading from left to right for the last three weeks instead of reading from right to left.

For Patrick, the course was indeed a long march.

Tai Chi Chuan Classics

I got on extremely well with Miss Chen. She went on a trip to China and learned some Tai Chi. When she came back, I got her interested in the Tai Chi Chuan Classics which she had never heard of. She really appreciated my introduction of the texts to her. Miss Chen helped me correct my first draft translation of the Classics.

Ticket Seller

Shortly after I received my Chinese Diploma, I met Mr Tang by chance one afternoon in the Strand. We had a drink together and he told me that the following weekend at a London Chinatown cinema his friend and therapist, Professor Lin Yun, head of the Black Hat Sect of Tibetan Tantric Buddhism was going to deliver two lectures.

The first lecture was about Qi energy on Saturday afternoon. The second lecture was about Feng Shui and would take place at 10 pm so that restaurant owners could attend. Professor Lin would deliver the lectures in Mandarin and they'd be translated into Cantonese.

I had nothing better to do so I went to the cinema and queued for a ticket. The attractive Chinese lady who was selling tickets started to tell me that the lecture was to be given in Chinese, but I told her I could understand Chinese, so she sold me a ticket.

As soon as the lecture was over, Mr Tang introduced the helpful ticket seller to me as his wife, Nancy. Mrs Tang said she had heard a lot about me and had been hoping to learn Tai Chi from me.

Nancy started having private lessons from me on a weekly basis and as well as paying me for tuition she helped me with my spoken and written Chinese. Miss Chen was a good friend of Mr Tang's wife Nancy.

After the course and with the help of these two ladies, I better understood the pictographic nature of characters, and their radicals and I realised I had effectively left the school of gradual enlightenment and was now a member of the school of sudden enlightenment – at least as far as Tai Chi was concerned.

Most translations of Tai Chi texts are appallingly inaccurate. It is not enough being a brilliant linguist if you don't have the practical knowledge like Sifu Cheng had.

Chinese boxer saying, "Learning boxing without training Kung (tough repetitive training) even if you do so until old, you will still be empty."

The same applies to learning Chinese.

Club of Dance and Self Defence

Thanks to Sifu Cheng misappropriating my gold, I needed to make some money. I read in the South London Press that The Club of Dance and Self Defence (CDSD) based in Elephant and Castle was looking for dance and martial arts instructors.

The Club was based in an old school. I found that all the folk on the premises were very pleasant Afro-Caribbeans. I was taken to see a gentleman called, Michael Jacques, from St Lucia, who was leader of a group of local social activists who had taken over the school in protest at the lack of amenities in the area.

Mike was delighted to hear that I had trained in Tai Chi in Hong Kong. He told me that he practiced boxing and Wado Ryu Karate and had wanted to learn Tai Chi for years. He asked when I could start. I told him Saturdays were good. Saturdays it was. Mike became my first student and proved to be a very capable martial artist. Nobody could beat Mike in pushing hands.

I had a few happy years teaching at the CDSD. I once heard an English martial arts teacher say that black people are no good at Tai Chi. Over the years, Mike and a host of black Tai Chi students have proven him wrong.

Mike is another person to whom I owe a karmic debt.

Epilogue

The memoirs of the Wild Colonial Boy end here.

Tai Chi is about change and *wu wei* (literally without action). If we are in a boat on a river and want to go upstream, we can row against the current or put up a sail and let the wind take us. Easy to say; difficult to do.

The 'uncarved block' is a Taoist metaphor for the callow youth before he is carved by change.

Despite everything, my arrogance, my stubbornness and my stupidity I'm proud to have been a 'wild colonial boy'. Reckon I need a bit more carving. Any offers?